The Teaching Manual
of
Perfect Summaries

His Divine Presence
The Divine Avataric World-Teacher
RUCHIRA AVATAR ADI DA SAMRAJ
Adi Da Samrajashram, 2008

The Teaching Manual
of
Perfect Summaries

The Revelation
of
The Preliminary
"Perfect Knowledge" Teachings of
His Divine Presence
The Divine Avataric World-Teacher
Ruchira Avatar Adi Da Samraj

THE DAWN HORSE PRESS
MIDDLETOWN, CALIFORNIA

NOTE TO THE READER

All who study the "Radical" Reality-Way of Adidam Ruchiradam or take up its practice should remember that they are responding to a Call to become responsible for themselves. They should understand that they, not Avatar Adi Da Samraj or others, are responsible for any decision they make or action they take in the course of their lives of study or practice.

The devotional, Spiritual, functional, practical, relational, and cultural practices and disciplines referred to in this book are appropriate and natural practices that are voluntarily and progressively adopted by members of the practicing congregations of Adidam (as appropriate to the personal circumstance of each individual). Although anyone may find these practices useful and beneficial, they are not presented as advice or recommendations to the general reader or to anyone who is not a member of one of the practicing congregations of Adidam. And nothing in this book is intended as a diagnosis, prescription, or recommended treatment or cure for any specific "problem", whether medical, emotional, psychological, social, or Spiritual. One should apply a particular program of treatment, prevention, cure, or general health only in consultation with a licensed physician or other qualified professional.

CONTENTS

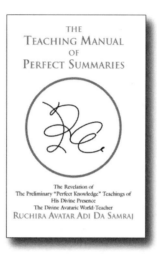

THE
TEACHING MANUAL
OF
PERFECT SUMMARIES

The Revelation of
The Preliminary "Perfect Knowledge" Teachings of
His Divine Presence
The Divine Avataric World-Teacher
RUCHIRA AVATAR ADI DA SAMRAJ

ABOUT THE COVER

The Image on the cover of *The Teaching Manual of Perfect Summaries* is an ink drawing by Ruchira Avatar Adi Da Samraj, made in 2008.

This drawing is an example of Avatar Adi Da's use of His "Orphic Font", which is a principal element of His Image-Art. In creating His Orphic Font (which may exist in an unlimited number of versions), Avatar Adi Da makes ink drawings corresponding to each of the letters of the Latin alphabet—drawings which may or may not have an evident visual similarity to the shapes of the alphabetical letters. The letters of the drawing on the cover of *The Teaching Manual of Perfect Summaries* correspond to capital "D" and lowercase "a", thus "spelling" His Principal Divine Name, "Da".

This book—the complete collection of Essays that comprise "The Teaching Manual of Perfect Summaries"—is a consummate Gift from His Divine Presence, the Divine Avataric World-Teacher, Ruchira Avatar Adi Da Samraj. The heart of this book, section II, contains essential Instruction that is recited daily for all student-beginners and beyond in the "Radical" Reality-Way of Adidam Ruchiradam. The additional Essays support this key Instruction, both in study and recitation. Avatar Adi Da Samraj has said that it is the preliminary practice of "Perfect Knowledge" (on the platform of "radical" devotion to Him and right-life obedience to Him) that enables the unique process of Transcendental Spirituality in the "Radical" Reality-Way of Adidam Ruchiradam. May all those who recognize Ruchira Avatar Adi Da Samraj prepare for this practice and receive the Gift of Awakening that He Is here to Offer.

Da Da Da

The Teaching Manual
of
Perfect Summaries

The Revelation
of
The Preliminary
"Perfect Knowledge" Teachings of
His Divine Presence
The Divine Avataric World-Teacher
Ruchira Avatar Adi Da Samraj

I

A Brief Introduction
To The Teaching Manual
of
Perfect Summaries

"The Teaching Manual of Perfect Summaries" is a short principal "Root"-Teaching Manual, in which I summarize My basic, preliminary "Perfect Knowledge" Teachings. I have Revealed and Given these preliminary "Perfect Knowledge" Teachings to be received daily via the practice of listening to formal recitations of this Teaching-Word of Mine. That practice of listening (and of subsequent tacit, intuitive, responsive coincidence with the Reality-Truth Indicated by My Word) is to be engaged daily and intensively by My every formally practicing First Congregation and Second Congregation devotee, previous to the "Perfect Practice"—from the point in each such individual's Second Congregation student-beginner practice of the only-by-Me Revealed and Given "Radical" Reality-Way of Adidam Ruchiradam when he or she is formally acknowledged to have demonstrated and proven (by means of in-life-manifested disposition and action, and not merely as a matter of "talk") entirely right, true, and real devotion to Me and full adaptation to the disciplines of right-life-obedience to Me. And practice in accordance with these, My preliminary "Perfect Knowledge" Teachings, is to be continuously engaged from then (and, in due course, within the formal practicing context of My First Congregation of devotees)—until My any such devotee enters, formally and fully, into the "Perfect Practice" of the only-by-Me Revealed and Given "Radical" Reality-Way of Adidam Ruchiradam (Which, as a totality, is the only-by-Me Revealed and Given Reality-Way of "Perfect Knowledge").

I am, now, and forever hereafter, always Calling and Expecting each and all of My formally (and yet preliminarily) practicing, and formally Initiated, First Congregation and fully adapted Second Congregation devotees to always practice in accordance with these preliminary "Root"-Teachings, while also always embracing and exercising (in specific accordance with their formally evaluated present-time demonstration of practice of the total by-Me-Revealed and by-Me-Given "Radical" Reality-Way of Adidam Ruchiradam) all of the other practices of the only-by-Me Revealed and only-by-Me Given "Radical" Reality-Way of Adidam Ruchiradam, Which is the total Reality-Way that I have Revealed and Given to all of My formally practicing First Congregation and Second Congregation devotees.

The many and various other Teachings and practices of the total by-Me-Revealed and by-Me-Given "Radical" Reality-Way of Adidam Ruchiradam encompass all of the practices of right devotion to Me, all of the practices of right-life obedience to Me, all of the practical and Transcendental Spiritual disciplines associated with the total process of the by-Me-Revealed and by-Me-Given "Radical" Reality-Way of Adidam Ruchiradam, and all of the Ultimate Teachings associated with the firmly and finally established "Perfect Practice" of the only-by-Me Revealed and Given "Radical" Reality-Way of Adidam Ruchiradam—Which "Perfect Practice" is the ultimate demonstration-context of the total by-Me-Revealed and by-Me-Given "Radical" Reality-Way of Adidam Ruchiradam.

The preliminary "Root"-Practice of the Reality-Way of "Perfect Knowledge" is—in perpetual conjunction with the always necessary foundation "Root"-Practice, of whole bodily devotional turning to Me—My most fundamental and essential basic Teaching, Revealed and Given for the sake of each and all of My formally practicing, but (also) yet maturing, devotees in the First and Second Congregations of Adidam Ruchiradam. Each and all of My such devotees should always, from the time of their formal Initiation into the preliminary "Root"-Practice of the (necessarily, Devotional) Reality-Way of "Perfect Knowledge", concentrate themselves in that preliminary "Root"-Practice, at every point in the total process of the by-Me-Revealed and by-Me-Given "Radical" Reality-Way of Adidam Ruchiradam, and in every context of moment to moment daily discipline and practice—until all preliminary forms of practice are, at last, transcended, in and by Means of the formal transition to the "Perfect Practice" of the only-by-Me Revealed and Given "Radical" Reality-Way of Adidam Ruchiradam.

Until the actual (non-preliminary, and Non-conditional) "Perfect Practice" of the only-by-Me Revealed and Given "Radical" Reality-Way of Adidam Ruchiradam is formally begun (in the case of My any formally fully practicing devotee—who must, necessarily, have been formally accepted as a full member of the Ruchira Sannyasin Order of Adidam Ruchiradam or as a full member of the Lay Renunciate Order of Adidam Ruchiradam), the (necessarily, formally embraced) preliminary "Perfect Knowledge" listening-practice of "Transcendental Root-Standing" should be constantly, intensively, and always tacitly engaged, both in the context of daily life and in the context of every formal occasion of meditation.

The preliminary "Perfect Knowledge" listening-practice of "Transcendental Root-Standing" is an Intrinsically searchless exercise—and not a seeking-"method" or a seeking-"technique". Thus, the right practice of "Transcendental Root-Standing" is, simply, to listen to the formal recitation of My Teaching-Word—and, rather than do something (as if My Instructions were prescribing a psycho-physical seeking-"method" or seeking-"technique"), to simply allow My Teaching-Word to be met intuitively, at heart, by a tacit, spontaneous "Root-Coincidence" with the by-Me-Indicated State of Self-Evident Reality-Truth Itself.

In any and every moment in which the tacit responsive process of "Transcendental Root-Standing" is active (as the "root"-form of the "conscious process"), even the verbal-mental exercise of Simple Name-Invocation of Me (Which is, in the daily culture of devotion to Me, the most basic ongoing form of the "conscious process") tends to become simple, tacit (or wordless and mindless) whole bodily devotional Communion with Me As I Am.

17

The preliminary "Perfect Knowledge" listening-practice of "Transcendental Root-Standing" is to be associated, as may in any moment be naturally required, with the formal exercise of the practices of "general conductivity"—and, in due course (in the context of practice within My First Congregation of devotees), with the devotional and Transcendental Spiritual practice of searchless Beholding of Me.

And, when the true, and mature, and Really Perfect—and, thus, Intrinsically Non-conditional, Non-egoic (or Anegoic), and, thus, neither "point-of-view"-based nor psycho-physically dependent—"Perfect Practice" of the only-by-Me Revealed and only-by-Me Given "Radical" Reality-Way of Adidam Ruchiradam is formally begun, the preliminary "Perfect Knowledge" listening-practice of "Transcendental Root-Standing" is to be relinquished, and replaced by the only-by-Me Revealed and only-by-Me Given "Perfect Practice" of "Radical Self-Abiding", and (subsequently) "general conductivity" is to be replaced, in formal occasions of "Perfect Contemplation" and in the circumstances of daily life, by "Radical Conductivity" (while, in the context of daily life, "general conductivity" is, also, as may be naturally required, to continue to be practiced, as previously).

II

The Teaching Manual
of
Perfect Summaries

The Preliminary Root-Practice
of
The Reality-Way of Perfect Knowledge

1.

The Five Reality-Teachings

Notice this:

1. You are <u>not</u> the one who wakes, or dreams, or sleeps.

2. You <u>Are</u> the actionless and formless Mere Witness of the three common states—of waking, dreaming, and sleeping—and of all the apparent contents and "experiences" associated with the three common states, of waking, and of dreaming, and of sleeping.

3. You are <u>not</u> the body, or the doer of action, or the doer of even <u>any</u> of the body's actions or functions.

4. You are <u>not</u> the mind, or the thinker, or the doer of even <u>any</u> of the actions or functions of mind or of body-mind.

5. No matter what arises—whether as or in the state of waking, or of dreaming, or of sleeping—you <u>Are</u> the actionless, and formless, and thought-free Mere Witness of attention itself, and of every apparent "object" of attention, and of any and every state of "experience", and of the entirety of whatever and <u>all</u> that arises.

Always intensively "consider" these Five Reality-Teachings.

Always intensively observe and notice every moment of your "experience"—whether waking, dreaming, or sleeping—and, thus and thereby, "consider" and test and directly prove these Five Reality-Teachings in the moment-to-moment of your every kind and state of "experience".

2.

The Intrinsic Self-Realization of Reality and Truth By Means of The Preliminary "Perfect Knowledge" Listening-Practice of Transcendental Root-Standing

The four principal faculties (or the psycho-physical functions of attention in association with body, emotion, mind, and breath) are constantly becoming associated with their various potential "objects" and states. Each faculty is, potentially, related to particular kinds of "objects" or "experiences" via itself, and, also, to particular states or "experiences" of itself.

Every kind of possible ("internal" or "external") "object", and every kind of ("internal" or "external") state, of each and any faculty is a kind of "knowledge"—or the "knowing" of a something (or of the whatever that is apparently, or conditionally, "known"). Thus, moment to moment (and, therefore, in any and every moment), the four principal faculties (or the psycho-physical functions of attention in association with body, emotion, mind, and breath) are involved in various modes—or states, or "objects", or events—of apparent (or conditional) "knowing".

The preliminary "Perfect Knowledge" listening-practice of "Transcendental Root-Standing" is a matter of moment to moment (and, thus, in every moment)—in every apparent condition of naturally noticing the "knowing" and the "known"—Intrinsically Self-Identifying (and Self-Standing As) the Intrinsically egoless "Perfect Knower" (Itself), Perfectly Prior to all "objects" and states of apparent (or conditional) "experience", and Perfectly Prior to the presumption of ego-"I" (or the separate "knowing-subject").

113100401 23/46 <> P1

<> 05/16/2008

3.

On The Intrinsic Transcending
of
The Fault of Objects

1. You are not any "<u>object</u>" that (apparently) arises.

2. Any and every "<u>object</u>" that apparently arises, arises conditionally—as and by means of conditional "cause" and conditional "effect".

3. No matter whatever apparently arises as an "<u>object</u>"— you are Whatever is not-an-"object".

4. Therefore, whatever (in any moment) apparently arises as an "<u>object</u>" (or apparently "objectively", over against the body or the mind)—<u>Be</u> (and, <u>only</u> <u>Thus</u>, Self-"Locate") Whatever is not-an-"object".

5. This is My Principal Instruction on the Preliminary "Perfect Knowledge" Listening-Practice of "Transcendental Root-Standing" exercised as Intrinsic Means for transcending the fault of "objects":

In any moment, and moment to moment, as and whenever any "object" (or any "objectively" arising anything, whether "internal" or "external" to the body or the mind) apparently arises—<u>Be</u> (and, only Thus, Self-"Locate") Whatever is not-an-"object".

4.

On The Intrinsic Transcending
of
The Fault of Knowledge
and The Known

1. You are not <u>any</u> whatever that (apparently) arises.

2. Whatever apparently arises, arises conditionally—as and by means of conditional "cause" and conditional "effect".

3. Whatever apparently arises is a whatever that is "known".

4. You are not any whatever that is (thus) "known".

5. Therefore, you are not the any "known"—whatever it appears to be.

6. Neither are you the (apparent) "knowledge" (or the apparent state of the "knowing") of any whatever that is (apparently) the "known".

7. No matter what apparently arises, you are the Intrinsically egoless "Perfect Knower"—Always Already Perfectly Prior to <u>it</u>.

8. No matter whatever is apparently the "known", you are the Intrinsically egoless "Perfect Knower"—Always Already Perfectly Prior to <u>it</u>.

9. No matter whatever is the apparent "knowledge" (or the apparent "knowing") of any whatever that is apparently the "known", you are the Intrinsically egoless "Perfect Knower"— Always Already Perfectly Prior to <u>it</u>.

10. No matter whatever apparently arises—as the "known", or as the any "knowing", or as the any "knowledge"—you are merely and only the Intrinsically egoless "Perfect Knower", Always Already Perfectly Prior to <u>it</u>.

11. Therefore, no matter whatever apparently arises—
Self-"Locate" the Intrinsically egoless "Perfect Knower"
only, and <u>Be</u> That.

12. This is My Principal Instruction on the Preliminary
"Perfect Knowledge" Listening-Practice of "Transcendental
Root-Standing" exercised as Intrinsic Means for transcending
the fault of "knowledge" and the "known":

**In any moment, and moment to moment, as
and whenever any whatever apparently arises—
Self-"Locate" the Intrinsically egoless "Perfect
Knower" only, and <u>Be</u> That.**

5.

On The Intrinsic Transcending
of
The Fault of Subjectivity

1. Every apparently (and conditionally) arising "object" is "known" as "object" only by an apparently (and conditionally) arising "knowing-subject" (or mode of egoic "self"-identity) that (itself) arises (as "knowing-subject") only in the instant of the "known-object"—and not previous (or otherwise prior) to the "known-object".

2. The "knowing-subject" (or the ego-"I") is always the subordinate of the "known-object".

3. The "known-object" implies and defines the nature and the very existence of its (always subsequent) egoic "knowing-subject".

4. The "knowing-subject" (or ego-"I") is the "effect" (or the reflective implication) of the "known-object".

5. In effect, the "knowing-subject" (or the presumed separate "self") is the "shadow" of the "known-object".

6. The "knowing-subject" (or the separate "self", as such) does not "cause" or precede the "known-object".

7. Both the "known-object" and its "shadow"—the ego-"I", or "knowing-subject", implied in the reflective context of the body-mind-complex—arise in the Always Already Perfectly Prior and Intrinsically egoless (or "subjectless") Self-Nature, Self-Condition, and Self-State of Reality Itself.

8. There are—in Reality Itself—no "subject-object" relations.

9. All apparently (and conditionally) arising "subject-object" relations (or "experiential" relational states) are (in Reality Itself) only "object-subject" conditions—or intrinsically

egoless appearances within the Always Already Perfectly Prior Context of Indivisible Reality Itself.

10. There are no ego-states—but, rather, there are only apparently (and merely conditionally) arising "objects" of presumed "knowledge".

11. Reality Itself (or Consciousness Itself) is not the "knowing-subject"—or the attentive "experiencer"—of any "known-object".

12. No mode of "knowing-subject" (or of attentively-"experiencing" ego-"I") is (itself) "known" as an "object" by Consciousness Itself (or Reality Itself).

13. Reality Itself—Self-Evident <u>As</u> the Self-Existing, Self-Radiant, and Intrinsically egoless Transcendental Spiritual Conscious Light That <u>Is</u> Consciousness Itself—<u>Is</u> the Mere and Non-separate Witness of any and every apparently and conditionally arising "object-subject" event.

14. Therefore, you are not the "knowing-subject" of any "known-object".

15. You <u>Are</u>, intrinsically and entirely, the Mere Witness (or egoless Transcendental Spiritual Conscious Light) of any and every kind of apparently (and conditionally) arising "knowing-subject" (or mode of egoic "self"-identity) and of any and every kind of apparently (and conditionally) arising "known-object".

16. Every kind and mode of apparently (and conditionally) arising "object" is "known" <u>as</u> "object" <u>only</u> to some kind and mode of apparently (and conditionally) arising "knowing-subject" (or conditionally presumed "self"-identity).

17. Modes (or apparent "knowledge-states") of the apparently (and conditionally) arising "experiential" body-mind-complex are the only possible "knowing-subject" (or ego-"I") of any apparently (and conditionally) arising "known-object".

18. No matter what "object" (whether apparently "internal" or apparently "external") becomes "known" to the ego-"I"—which is only and entirely the conditionally arising body-mind-complex itself—you Are only the One, and Indivisible, and Non-separate, and Intrinsically egoless, and, altogether, Perfect Transcendental Spiritual Conscious Light, Which is Self-Evident As the Self-Nature, Self-Condition, and Self-State of Witness-only, and Which Is Reality Itself (Always Already Perfectly Prior to "knowing-subject" and "known-object").

19. Therefore, in any moment, no matter what arises as apparent "knowing-subject" or apparent "known-object"—Be (and, only Thus, Self-"Locate") the Inherently Free-Standing and Perfectly Free Witness-only, Which Is Consciousness (or Transcendental Self-Awareness) Itself, Self-Evident As Love-Bliss (or As the Intrinsic Energy, Current, Self-Light, or Transcendental Spiritual Self-"Brightness" of Self-Aware Consciousness Itself).

20. This is My Principal Instruction on the Preliminary "Perfect Knowledge" Listening-Practice of "Transcendental Root-Standing" exercised as Intrinsic Means for transcending the fault of "subjectivity":

In any moment, and moment to moment, as and whenever the "subjective" feeling, or the egoic thought, or the however felt "self"-idea of "I" arises— Be the Witness-only, and, only Thus, Self-"Locate" the Intrinsically Self-Evident Self-Nature, Self-Condition, and Self-State That is neither the "knowing-subject" nor the "known-object" of or to or as any separate one at all.

45

6.

On The Intrinsic Transcending
of
The Fault of Attention
(or Point of View)

1. All forms and modes of "subject-object-knowledge" (or all mere ideas) about Reality (Itself, and altogether) are merely mental (or even total psycho-physical) constructs— necessarily based upon the fault of "point of view" (or of egoic "self-location" in time and space).

2. The fault of "point of view" is (inclusively, and altogether) the fault of "objects", the fault of "knowledge" and the "known", and the fault of "subjectivity" (or of the illusory presumption of the substantial, independent, separate, and irreducible "self"-existence of a "point-of-view-self").

3. The arising of the illusory presumption of a "point-of-view-self" (or "knowing-subject") is always tacitly indicated by the arising of functional attention.

4. Attention is the first representation of the ego-"I"— or the total psycho-physical "self"-contraction upon the presumption of separate "point of view".

5. Attention is the essential form of the presumed "knowing-subject".

6. Attention is the functional means whereby the intrinsically egoless perception-body contacts the inherently indivisible field of conditionally arising perceptible appearances.

7. Attention is the functional means whereby the intrinsically egoless perception-body identifies and individuates all its "known-objects".

8. Attention is the functional doorway to the "exterior" field of potential "known-objects"—and attention is, also, the functional doorway to the "interior" domain of the "shadow", or the "object"-defined "knowing-self" of all-reflecting egoity.

49

9. Attention is the all-and-All-limiting functional agent of "point of view".

10. Attention is the fault whereby Reality (Itself, and altogether) is dis-"Located" from (and by) any and every "point of view".

11. Therefore, how is Reality (Itself, and altogether) to be "Located", participated in, understood, and Realized—or "Perfectly Known"?

12. Reality (Itself—and altogether, or As "It" Is in the context of all-and-All apparent conditional arising) Is Always Already (or Inherently) Beyond and Prior to any "point of view" (and all possible "points of view").

13. Reality (Itself, and altogether) Is Inherently and Perfectly Un-"known" and Un-"knowable" as an "object" of "point of view".

14. That Which Is Inherently and Perfectly Un-"known" and Un-"knowable" as an "object" of "point of view" Is Realizable only by and As Perfect Ignorance—or Intrinsically egoless Not-"knowing".

15. Perfect Ignorance, or Intrinsically egoless Not-"knowing", Is "Perfect Knowledge".

16. Perfect (and Perfectly egoless) Ignorance, or Perfect Not-"knowing", Is "Perfect Knowledge" of Reality (Itself, and altogether) As "It" Is.

17. "Perfect Knowledge" (or Perfect Not-"knowing") Is the Intrinsically Self-Evident (Perfectly Prior, and Intrinsically egoless, and Intrinsically Perfect) Self-Nature, Self-Condition, and Self-State of Tacitly Self-Abiding As Is—no matter what (apparently and conditionally) arises or does not arise.

18. Only "Perfect Knowledge" (or Perfect Not-"knowing")—and not any kind or mode of mere conditional, or idea-based, or "subject-object"-based "knowledge"—can Really (or in and As Reality) "Know" (and Be the, necessarily, Intrinsically egoless "Perfect Knower" of) Reality (Itself, and altogether).

19. "Perfect Knowledge" and the "Perfect Knower" are of a suprarational (or only and Perfectly Reality-Based) Nature (or of the Nature of Perfect Ignorance)—and not merely of either a conventionally "rational" (and, thus, merely mind-based) or (otherwise) "irrational" (or "anti-rational", or otherwise mentally-deficient, mentally-deranged, or mentally-deceived) nature.

20. "Perfect Knowledge" Is only the "Perfect Knower" Itself.

21. To Merely Be the "Perfect Knower" (Itself) Is "Perfect Knowledge" Itself.

22. The "Perfect Knower" Is the "Perfect Knowledge" (or Perfect Self-Apprehension, or Perfect Self-Apperception) of Itself.

23. The "Perfect Knower" Is the "Perfect Knowledge" (or Perfect Self-Apprehension, or Perfect Self-Apperception) of all-and-All that arises conditionally to Intrinsically egoless and Perfect Not-"knowing".

24. The "Perfect Knowledge" of all-and-All that arises conditionally Is Perfect (and Always Already Priorly egoless) Self-Recognition of all-and-All in, of, and As the "Perfect Knower" Itself—Such That all-and-All is (Thus) Self-Recognized As Being Thus (or As Being Only the Perfectly egoless "Perfect Knower" Itself).

25. The only-by-Me Revealed and Given Reality-Way of "Perfect Knowledge" (Which <u>Is</u> the only-by-Me Revealed and Given Reality-Way of Divine Ignorance, or of Perfectly egoless Not-"knowing") <u>Is</u> the Persistent Self-"Exercise"— and, in due course, the "Perfect (Transcendental Spiritual) Practice"—of the Intrinsic Self-Apprehension (or the Intuitive Self-Apperception) of the Always Already Perfectly Prior, Intrinsically egoless, and Perfectly Indivisible Self-Nature, Self-Condition, and Self-State of the Perfectly Non-separate "Perfect Knower", Which <u>Is</u> the Perfect Self-Nature, Self-Condition, and Self-State of all-and-All.

26. Therefore, the Preliminary "Perfect Knowledge" Listening-Practice of "Transcendental Root-Standing" is epitomized by the <u>Tacit</u> "Root"-transcending of "point of view"—and the necessary "Event" (or actionless and Non-conditional "Happen") of the Tacit (or Perfectly Intrinsic) "Root"-transcending of "point of view" <u>Is</u> the Intrinsic Self-Apperception of Intrinsically "objectless" and "attentionless" Consciousness Itself (or the Mere Witness Itself), Which Intrinsic Self-Apperception <u>Is</u> (Itself) the Intrinsically egoless Self-"Exercise" of the Always Already Perfectly Prior (and, Thus, Perfectly searchless, or mentally, emotionally, and physically actionless) "Root"-transcending of <u>attention</u> (itself).

27. This is My Principal Instruction on the Preliminary "Perfect Knowledge" Listening-Practice of "Transcendental Root-Standing" exercised as Intrinsic Means for transcending the fault of "attention" (or "point of view"):

In any moment, and moment to moment, as and whenever and toward whatever attention (itself) arises, Tacitly and Intrinsically (and, Thus, <u>not</u> in a dissociatively introversive seeking-manner) Self-Apperceive (or Intrinsically Self-"Locate") <u>That</u> In, From, Of, and (<u>Therefore</u>) <u>As</u> Which attention (itself) is arising—and (Thus and Thereby) Merely <u>Be</u> the Witness-only, Always Already Self-Abiding <u>In</u> and <u>As</u> the Always Already Priorly egoless, and Intrinsically "point-of-view"-less, and Perfectly "objectless", and Perfectly searchless Not-"knowing" That <u>Is</u> Consciousness Itself, no matter what arises or does not arise.

7.

<u>Is</u> Happen

W hat is <u>not</u> an "object"?
What is <u>not</u> the "known"?
What is <u>not</u> the "knowing" of an "object"?
What is <u>not</u> the "knowledge" of an "object"?

What is <u>not</u> the "knowing-subject" (or the "knowing-self") of any "known-object"?

What <u>Is</u> the "Perfect Knower"—Prior to any "known-object", Prior to any "knowing", Prior to any "knowledge", and Prior to any "knowing-subject" (or "self" that "knows")?

Wherein, Wherefrom, Whereof, and (Therefore) <u>As</u> What does attention (itself) arise?

What <u>Is</u> Always Already Prior to attention (itself)—even in any and every moment in which attention arises and associates itself with any and every kind of "object"?

"Locate" <u>That</u>.

<u>Be</u> <u>That</u>.

Only <u>Thus</u> (by <u>Being</u> <u>That</u>), Self-"Locate" <u>That</u> (<u>As</u> <u>Is</u>).

<u>That</u> <u>Is</u> <u>That</u>.

<u>That</u> <u>Is</u> "It".

<u>That</u> <u>Is</u> All.

<u>That</u> <u>Is</u> all-in-All.

<u>That</u> <u>Is</u> all-and-All.

<u>Is</u> <u>Happen</u> <u>That</u> <u>Is</u>.

III

The Searchless and Acausally Awakened Preliminary Listening-Practice of Perfect Knowledge

The preliminary listening-practice of "Perfect Knowledge" is not any kind of "technique"—not any kind of program of seeking, or strategic (and would-be "causative") effort of body or mind—to be exercised by My devotees.

The preliminary listening-practice of "Perfect Knowledge" is not even any kind of "technique" (or "method" of meditation) that people might attempt to derive from My "Teaching Manual of Perfect Summaries".

Rather, the preliminary listening-practice of "Perfect Knowledge" is simply the Tacit Self-Apprehension of Reality Itself—Which becomes spontaneously Self-Evident in the circumstance of whole-bodily-attentive (and truly turned-to-Me) listening to My Word of "Perfect Knowledge".

The practice to be exercised by My devotees, in response to listening to (or, otherwise, studying or "considering") My Word of "Perfect Knowledge", is simply the (always more and more profoundly actualized) searchless whole bodily devotional Beholding of Me.

My devotees will, inevitably, "consider" My Word of "Perfect Knowledge" in the circumstance of moment to moment living, and will, inevitably, call My Word of "Perfect Knowledge" to mind (even, at times, in the circumstance of formal meditation). Such "consideration" and calling-to-mind is certainly relevant to the practice of the only-by-Me Revealed and Given "Radical" Reality-Way of Adidam Ruchiradam—but such "consideration" and calling-to-mind is not, itself, the right and true listening-practice associated with My Word of "Perfect Knowledge".

The fundamental mode of receiving My Word of "Perfect Knowledge" (or, indeed, My Word of Instruction altogether) is, literally, to listen to It. My devotees can (and should), of course, read and study My Word silently—but the primal situation is that of listening to the recitation of My Word. In particular, My fully adapted (and yet-maturing) devotees should listen to the recitation of My "Teaching Manual of Perfect Summaries"—and, as they listen to It, My thus listening devotees should simply allow the Self-Evidence of Tacit Self-Apprehension of egoless Reality Itself to Demonstrate Itself. The ongoing Event (or moment to moment, and day after day, process) of That Tacit Self-Apprehension inevitably frees up the faculties more and more profoundly, in the truly attentive and freely surrendered-to-Me manner, and allows always deeper Communion with Me (As I Am) to Self-Manifest—as a tacit and Acausally Self-Revealed demonstration, rather than as some kind of seeking-exercise, or seeking-"method", that intends to "cause" (or egoically, and psycho-physically, "self-create") "Perfect Knowledge" as a goal, or a result, of "self"-effort.

What, exactly, is the preliminary listening-practice of My "Perfect Knowledge" Teaching? The preliminary listening-practice of My "Perfect Knowledge" Teaching is not (itself) an exercise, or a purposive effort to achieve (or psycho-physically "cause") "Perfect Knowledge". Rather, the preliminary listening-practice of My "Perfect Knowledge" Teaching is to be brought into the context of every moment of life and meditation by simply listening to My Word of "Perfect Knowledge", listening to My Direct Self-Confessions and Self-Revelatory Statements of Self-Evident Reality-Truth.

When, in My "Teaching Manual of Perfect Summaries", I Instruct My devotees to "Self-'Locate' Whatever is not-an-'object'" (and so forth), those Instructions are Self-Confessional Admonitions from Me, relative to Which there should simply be an immediate tacit agreement—or a thoughtless, or non-mentalized, recognition of coincidence, rather than a subsequent action in time, or a psycho-physically strategic and would-be "causative" effort of intentionality. In Giving those Admonitions, I am not Calling My devotees to make the "remembering" of the Admonitions into some kind of exercise whereby effort is made to seek to "Self-'Locate' Whatever is not-an-'object'" (and so forth). Thus, the preliminary listening-practice of "Perfect Knowledge" is always (simply) the <u>Tacit</u> Self-Apprehension of Reality Itself—through whole-bodily-attentive (and, thus, "self"-surrendered) <u>listening</u> to My Word of "Perfect Knowledge".

The right and true preliminary listening-practice of "Perfect Knowledge" is never an exercise of seeking.

Rather, the preliminary listening-practice of "Perfect Knowledge" is, simply, the Tacit Self-Apprehension of the <u>Self-Evident</u> <u>Condition</u> of Reality Itself.

The Intrinsically egoless Self-Nature, Self-Condition, and Self-State of Reality Itself is not something you will "achieve" (or "self-cause") through a progressive process of psycho-physical effort.

The Intrinsically egoless Self-Nature, Self-Condition, and Self-State of Reality Itself is, in any given moment of listening to Me, either Self-Evident or not.

The Means I Give are Acausal.

If you are My devotee, you simply turn (responsively) to Me and whole bodily listen to My Word—and, thus, the Tacit Self-Apprehension of Reality Itself occurs, in exact coincidence with devotional resort to My Person.

The demonstration of the preliminary listening-practice of "Perfect Knowledge" is simply the devotional response to Me—the turning of the psycho-physical faculties to Me, and, in due course, the "self"-surrendered (and more and more truly searchless) whole bodily Beholding of Me.

Thus, the preliminary "Perfect Knowledge" listening-practice is not a separate and independent practice.

Rather, the preliminary "Perfect Knowledge" listening-practice is one with the totality of the by-Me-Revealed and by-Me-Given foundation practice of the "Radical" Reality-Way of Adidam Ruchiradam.

The totality of the by-Me-Revealed and by-Me-Given foundation practice of the "Radical" Reality-Way of Adidam

THE TEACHING MANUAL OF PERFECT SUMMARIES

Ruchiradam is "radical" devotion to Me, right-life obedience to Me, and (thus) whole-bodily-attentive listening to My preliminary "Perfect Knowledge" Teachings.

That totality of foundation practice also (eventually) continues in the Transcendental Spiritual (and, necessarily, formal renunciate) course of the "Radical" Reality-Way of Adidam Ruchiradam—until there is the by-My-Divine-Avataric-Transcendental-Spiritual-Grace-Given entrance into the "Perfect Practice" (and, in due course, the seventh stage Demonstration) of the only-by-Me Revealed and Given "Radical" Reality-Way of Adidam Ruchiradam.

IV

<u>A</u>s "It" <u>I</u>s

1.

I n Reality As "It" Is, there is neither "knowing-subject" nor "known-object". In Reality As "It" Is, there are no "objects" arising (as the "known", or as "knowledge", or, otherwise, to yet be "known")—and, in Reality As "It" Is, there are no "knowing-subjects" (or "knowledge-bearing-egos") arising (as the "knower", or the would-be "knower", of "objects"). Rather, all conditionally apparent "objects" and "subjects" are (as such) mere mental (or even total psycho-physical) constructs, superimposed upon the Intrinsic (and Intrinsically "objectless", or "differenceless", and "subjectless", or egoless, and all-conditional-"knowledge"-transcending) Transcendental Spiritual Self-Nature (or Intrinsically Self-Evident Self-Condition, and Intrinsically egoless Self-State) of Reality (Itself, and altogether).

That Which seems to become "objects" is an Indivisible (or Inherently Non-differentiated, or "differenceless") Field of merely apparent conditional arising. That Field is not sep-arate from the Perfectly Prior Self-Nature, Self-Condition, and Self-State of Reality Itself—nor is there, in and As Reality Itself, any arising of independent "object-things". Reality Itself—and the Reality-Field of apparent conditionally-arising phenomena that Is Not "different" from "It"—Is The One and Irreducibly Indivisible and Perfectly Non-differentiated Field That Is As Is.

The human body arises non-"differently" in That Primary Field. The Intrinsically (or always Priorly) egoless body is a conditionally apparent mechanism of perception and response. There is no "separate self inside the body"—and the body itself is not a "self". Rather, the body is an irreducibly com-plex collection of would-be-cooperative mechanisms—alto-gether, not merely separate, and not "selfed", and not reducible to an idea, or to the thinking-process, or even to a precise interior "locus of being". The body is, fundamentally, a complex cooperative of perception, always "located" in a general position (but not as a mere "point") in space, and never in or of a fixed "location" in time. As the Inherently Non-differentiated Field of perception and the intrinsically egoless body come into conjunction with one another, the Indivisible Field is perceived from the general "location" of the body in time and space. That happening becomes the bodily-organized perception of "objects". The particularity of "objects" <u>reflected</u> in and of the body is a perceptual-feedback circumstance that, in the bodily context, may be presumed (and, conventionally, or egoically, is invariably presumed) to <u>imply</u> (at the bodily-presumed "point" of perception) a "point-of-view-subject", or "knowing-self". It is only in this bodily perception-conjunction—in which "objects" have <u>already</u> (apparently) arisen in the Non-differentiated Field and become reflected in the bodily perception-complex— that a "knowing-self" (or separate "self", or ego-"I") is "internally" (or mentally), and (altogether) psycho-physically, presumed to be implied (and, <u>thus</u>, to <u>actually</u> and <u>Really exist</u> <u>as such</u>).

There is—in Reality <u>As</u> "It" <u>Is</u>—no ego in, or behind, or appearing as the body. The event of body-conjunction with the Non-differentiated Field naturally becomes the selective perception of apparently arising forms—and that perception may seem (or be responsively presumed) to imply that the body (felt as a "point of view" in time and space) is a "knowing-self". However, this "knowing-self" (or ego-"I") is merely a presumption—a mere reflection (or "shadow") of "objects". Because of the natural (all-reflecting) perceptual conjunction between the body and the "experiential objects" in the otherwise Non-differentiated (or Indivisible) Field, the bodily perception-process is (mistakenly) presumed to <u>be</u> (or, altogether, imply or suggest) a ("self-objectified") "knowing-subject".

In Reality, there is (in the apparent context of all conditional arising) only the intrinsically egoless happening of perceiving-bodies arising—indeed, only the intrinsically egoless happening of all the apparent phenomena of conditionality. In Reality, all that is perceivable and all mechanisms (or bodies) of possible perception arise indivisibly and egolessly, as an intrinsically and irreducibly indivisible and egoless totality. In the event of the conjunction of bodies and the egoless happening altogether, there is the reflection—or the "shadowing" presumption of separate "self" in time and space. The ego-presumption comes about as a result of the natural conjunction between the body and the Non-differentiated Field of perception—but the ego-presumption is (as such) an illusion, or a mere mental (or even total psycho-physical) convention of "self-objectification", without necessity (or Really-"objective" existence), but, also, always associated with the concrete suffering of egoic consequences.

There is no ego-"I" in the body.

The body itself is intrinsically egoless and non-separate.

There is no separateness in the Field.

The presumption of separate ego-"I" and the presumption of separate "objects" is simply that—a presumption (or a mental, or even total psycho-physical, construct). That presumption can (therefore) be observed, understood, and transcended. However, the transcending of that presumption is not merely an intellectual matter. Fundamentally, the transcending of that presumption is a Transcendental Spiritual matter. The Non-differentiated and Indivisible Current of Self-Radiance That is the Transcendental Spiritual Context of the Field of happening is the Reality-Means whereby the limitation of presumed ego-"I" is transcended.

The preliminary listening-practice of "Perfect Knowledge" is a process that begins and (always, thereafter) proceeds in the context of devotional recognition-response to Me and whole bodily devotional turning to Me—in which context the presumed "point-of-view"-position <u>and</u> the total psycho-physical "self"-contraction that (both together, and altogether) <u>is</u> egoity is transcended in Transcendental Spiritual (and total psycho-physical) devotional Communion with Me. In due course, devotional recognition-response to Me and whole bodily devotional turning to Me becomes the circumstance of devotional <u>and</u> Transcendental Spiritual Communion with Me, wherein the comprehensive fault of ego-"I" is altogether (intrinsically) transcended. In that transcending, the limiting power of "knowing-subject" and its separate "known-objects" is transcended. Ultimately, this process becomes the "Perfect (Transcendental Spiritual) Practice" of the only-by-Me Revealed and Given (and, uniquely, seventh stage) "Radical" Reality-Way of Adidam Ruchiradam.

2.

During the period of the European Renaissance, there was a profound struggle to come to terms with the notion that the nature of the universe was not as it had previously been presumed to be. The "old view" had the Earth at the center of everything. In the period of the European Renaissance, people had to come to terms with the notion, based on physical (perceptual) observation, that the Earth (along with the other planets of the solar system) revolves around the Sun.

The "old view" did not rightly represent Reality-Truth—but neither does the "new view" rightly represent Reality-Truth. In either case (whether "old" or "new"), if the "point of view" were shifted so much as a hair's breadth to the left or the right, the universe so described would no longer exist.

Reality <u>Itself</u> is not any "view", or in any "point of view". Reality Itself is not merely the idea of "God creating and running the universe". Rather, Reality—Itself, and in the context of all conditionally arising appearances—is <u>Inherently</u>

Divine (or egoless, Indivisible, Absolute, Transcendental, Spiritual, and Perfect) in Nature.

In Reality Itself, there is no center. In Reality Itself, there are no spheres within the sphere. And, yet (paradoxically), there is the appearance of conditionally arising events.

Participation in the appearance of conditionally arising events can either be done on the egoless Basis of Reality Itself or on the basis of the illusion of egoity.

Either there is the Enlightened Life (of egoless Self-Illumination in and by Reality Itself) or there is the mummery of "Narcissus" in ego-"world".

There are no other choices.

3.

People are full of habits—full of adaptation and presumption—based on living as if there actually were a separate "self", associated with a "world" of separate others and separate "objects" of all kinds (including "internal objects" as well as "external objects"). The egoic life is built upon this illusion—and a very complex pattern develops on the basis of this illusory presumption of universal separateness, of separate "objects", and of separate "self". That complex pattern is bondage.

People live habitually on the basis of this pattern. They are patterned by this pattern. In fact, there is nothing but this pattern—patterning itself. Therefore, the "world" of egos is a mummery, an automaticity—conjunctions of mere patterns mechanically producing permutations of mere patterns.

The real practice of the only-by-Me Revealed and Given "Radical" Reality-Way of Adidam Ruchiradam is a profound matter of turning beyond ego-patterning, and being released of ego-patterning, by entering into profoundest devotional (and, in due course, Transcendental Spiritual) Communion with Me.

The "knowing-subject" (or ego-"I") is the "shadow" (or "Narcissistic" reflection) of the "known-object". The "knowing-subject" is the "shadow" of all "experience" that is presumed to be happening to a "point of view"—like a planet presumed to be the "center" of the Sun's revolutions. The "knowing-subject" is an illusion, an illusory "self". The "world" of human mummery is made of that illusion. The human ego-"world" is a mummery played on an illusion of "centered-ness" (or the illusion of "point of view"). The "world" of conditionally apparent "experience" is very (and even, to any "point of view", incomprehensibly) complex, because it becomes multiplied within itself through all kinds of conjunctions played on time and space—thus producing a complex human life, and a complex totality of human "world"-pattern.

Real practice of the only-by-Me Revealed and Given "Radical" Reality-Way of Adidam Ruchiradam is a profound process of going beyond ego-patterning—actually going beyond it, shedding it, turning from it, and (instead) turning to Me and living in devotional Communion with Me. If the Realization of Reality Itself is your true motive and impulse, your life can be made profound and egolessly one-pointed. If the Realization of Reality Itself is not your motive and impulse, your life will remain essentially superficial and, generally, scattered.

The ruling presumption within the human ego-"world" (or the human mummery-"world") is of a separate "self" in a "world" of differences. In Reality, there is no separate "self", and there are no differences. However, the Realization of Reality Itself is not about dissociation from the apparent context of the "world". Rather, the Realization of Reality Itself is (most ultimately) a matter of Self-Abiding Divine Self-Recognition of the "world" in (and As) Reality Itself. Thus, the Realization of Reality Itself is (most ultimately) a matter of the utter transcending of the separate-"self"-principle, and the Self-Abiding Divine Self-Recognition of the "world" as a Non-differentiated Field of No-"difference", or of Indivisible and Non-differentiated Reality.

The only-by-Me Revealed and Given seventh stage Realization is not a matter of "retreating" into the "knowing-self" at its depth—nor is the only-by-Me Revealed and Given seventh stage Realization a matter of "escaping" from the "world". In the only-by-Me Revealed and Given "Radical" Reality-Way of Adidam Ruchiradam, there is no requirement or necessity to "escape" from the "world", nor is there any requirement or necessity to somehow (strategically, and egoically) accomplish the "self-destruction" of the ego-"self". The seventh stage Realization is the Realization that there is no separate "self" and there is no field of differences. You do not have to disappear from here in order to Find egolessness and No-"difference". There is always already no ego-"I" and no "difference" here.

The only-by-Me Revealed and Given seventh stage Realization is not a trance-state, not any kind of state in which perceptual awareness is merely suspended. Rather, the only-by-Me Revealed and Given seventh stage Realization is a State of Perfect Divine Self-Recognition, Perfect (or Prior, rather than "achieved") egolessness—in Which, even in the context of the apparent event of the "world" and of human existence, there is no separateness, no separate "self" (or "knowing-self", or ego-"I"), no "difference", no "objects", no others, no otherness, and no relatedness (or "subject-object"-bondage).

From the egoic perspective, it is impossible to comprehend how life could go on if you were to come to the point where there is no ego and no "difference". Of course, this is not something that you can "figure out". When there is Most Perfect Realization of Reality Itself, it is always already "figured out". The Realization of Reality Itself is a Transcendental Spiritual matter, a matter of profundity-beyond-mind.

Realization of Reality Itself is not a matter of attaining some artificial condition, or some state of suspension, or some illusion. Rather, Realization of Reality Itself is a matter of Realizing What <u>Is</u> Always Already The Case, even in the apparent context of the "world" arising.

There is no separate "self", no mind, and no "difference".

There is only a Spontaneous Happening.

That <u>Is</u> "It"—<u>As</u> "It" <u>Is</u>.

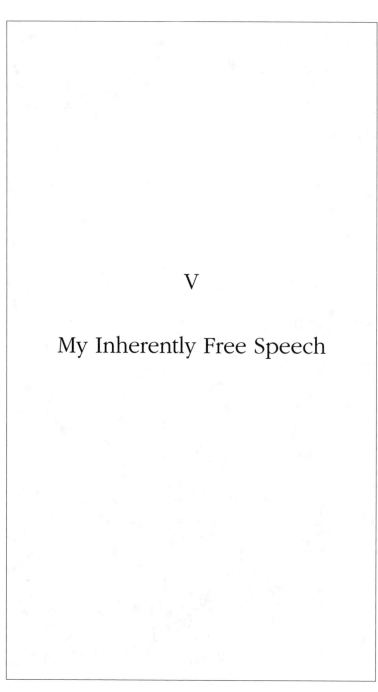

V

My Inherently Free Speech

1.

The only-by-Me Revealed and Given "Radical" Reality-Way of Adidam Ruchiradam—as an <u>always</u> "radical" (or "at-the-root") demonstration-process that culminates in the only-by-Me Revealed and Given "Perfect Practice"—will (and must) forever remain as It has been fully Described by Me. And the true, right, and necessary context of practice of the only-by-Me Revealed and Given "Radical" Reality-Way of Adidam Ruchiradam will always be the right, true, and full practice of "radical" devotion to Me, ego-transcending "self"-discipline (or right-life obedience to Me), and "Perfect Knowledge".

Nevertheless, even in all the while in which My devotees are yet maturing in the demonstration of that always "radical" (or "at-the-root") process, I must <u>always</u> Speak My Own (seventh stage) State of Realization. And I must <u>always</u> Make Direct Utterance from, and in, and <u>As</u> That State—openly, and even from the beginning of the process of the yet maturing demonstration of the (always "radical", or "at-the-root") "preliminary" practice of any and all of My devotees. Such Utterance is the Inherently Free Speech of My seventh stage Realization <u>Itself</u>, expressed through the Perfect Self-Revelation and Perfect Instruction that correspond to That Realization. And I must Give That Instruction <u>openly</u>—to <u>everyone</u>—such that My "Radical" (or Perfectly "At-the-Root") Teachings of "Perfect Knowledge" and "Perfect Practice" are, always and in fact, the <u>foundation</u> of the only-by-Me Revealed and Given "Radical" Reality-Way of Adidam Ruchiradam, even beginning in the foundation (Second Congregation student-beginner) stage of Its formal practice by any and all of My formally practicing devotees.

I am always already Moved to Speak <u>only</u> the Word of My Own Divine Self-Realization—and to Speak <u>only</u> of the

"Perfect Knowledge" practice that coincides with That Realization Itself. I am always already Moved to Speak the Intrinsic Truth of Reality Itself, and in plainest terms, Avatarically Self-Revealing My Own State and Person As I Am—and spontaneously Revealing Teachings That Come from That State of Realization Itself.

All that I have Taught—the entire "Radical" Reality-Way of Adidam Ruchiradam—has Come from That Inherently Perfect State of Realization. Thus, in Making My Revelation of Adidam Ruchiradam, I have been Avatarically Self-Revealing Myself—and My Divine Avataric Self-Revelation-Work can (and must) continue in perpetuity.

I am entirely Moved, as a matter of Heart-Necessity, to Self-Manifest My Own State, and to Make Utterance of the Reality-Way That Perfectly corresponds with My Own Most Perfect Realization. That Instructive Utterance of Mine is the Divine Avataric Self-Revelation of the only-by-Me Revealed and Given "Perfect Knowledge" and "Perfect Practice" of Adidam Ruchiradam—Which "Perfect Knowledge" and "Perfect Practice" is not merely a "self"-applied philosophy and technique, but It is the Reality-Way of "Perfect Knowledge" of Me, and of the "Perfect Practice" of devotion to Me As I Am.

For anyone to fully practice My Perfect Reality-Way, he or she must be My Perfect devotee, having fulfilled the entire course of the "Radical" Reality-Way of Adidam Ruchiradam as I have Revealed and Given It in Its totality—always based in right devotional recognition-response to Me, and in fullest practice of whole bodily devotional turning to Me. There is no doubt about this. That is an absolute necessity.

Nevertheless, I have also Revealed and Given a preliminary mode of "Perfect Knowledge" listening-practice to all My formally practicing and rightly devotionally qualified (First and Second Congregation) devotees who have not yet matured into the "Perfect Practice" Itself. Therefore, as soon as My any Second Congregation student-beginner devotee is formally acknowledged as having <u>demonstrated</u> and <u>proven</u> right, true, and real devotion to Me, he or she is Called and Expected, by Me, to embrace the daily, and, effectively, moment to moment, preliminary "Perfect Knowledge" listening-practice of "Transcendental Root-Standing".

Until My any Second Congregation novice student-beginner devotee has fully adapted to the primary practice of "radical" devotion to Me and the by-Me-Given disciplines of right life, he or she should simply study "the Five Reality-Teachings" I have herein Revealed and Given. Once My any Second Congregation novice student-beginner devotee is formally acknowledged to be fully adapted to the practice of "radical" devotion to Me and right-life obedience to Me, and (also) demonstrates signs of readiness to embrace the "Perfect Knowledge" listening-practice, he or she (as My formally fully adapted student-beginner devotee) is Initiated into the <u>preliminary</u> listening-practice of "Perfect Knowledge" and begins to adapt to the preliminary listening-practice of "Perfect Knowledge" both in formal meditation occasions and in daily life. Therefore, it is <u>only</u> on the basis of the formal full student-beginner (and, thus, Second Congregation) demonstration of adaptation to the foundation devotional and right-life practice of the only-by-Me Revealed and Given "Radical" Reality-Way of Adidam Ruchiradam that the <u>preliminary</u> listening-practice of "Perfect Knowledge" is Given, by Me, for the practice, and constant "consideration", and constant exercise of My <u>every</u> thus rightly qualified devotee—and that preliminary listening-practice is always to be engaged on the basis of the fullest right practice of the (necessarily, devotional) "Radical" Reality-Way of Adidam Ruchiradam, as I have otherwise already fully Given It.

I <u>Am</u> the Truth <u>Itself</u>—and I <u>Am</u> <u>here</u>. I must Speak This Truth. I must perpetually, constantly, and urgently Speak My Word of Self-Revelation, and My Communication of "Perfect Knowledge" and the "Perfect Practice"—even to everyone, because everyone can understand My Reality-Word of the "Perfect Knowledge" and the "Perfect Practice" of Truth. It is simply that, until anyone is fully matured in what is preliminary, he or she cannot yet Realize the Truth Perfectly.

I have been Self-Revealing the Perfect Truth all the while of My Avatarically-Born Divine Life in this "world". And I have, over time, Completely Uttered the "Perfect Knowledge" and "Perfect Practice" Teachings. It is simply that—now that the Submission I made in order to Teach has become a Complete Teaching-Revelation—I have (now, and forever hereafter) no inclination but to Reveal Myself Perfectly, As I Am, without any further Submission or Subordination of Myself to devotees and the "world". Indeed, now, and forever hereafter, I have no choice but to Self-Reveal Myself As I Am. That Is Who I Am. Therefore, I am Moved only to Make Utterance of My Own State of Self-Realization, and of the principles of practice that correspond to My Own Perfect State of Self-Realization. To do that, then, I must simply be Communicating the Reality-Way of "Perfect Knowledge" and, ultimately, of the "Perfect Practice" of the "Radical" Reality-Way of Adidam Ruchiradam.

Even though I Speak the "Perfect Knowledge" of Truth, and a practice that, ultimately, is in the mode of the "Perfect Practice" of Truth (which practice is the ultimate form of practice in the only-by-Me Revealed and Given "Radical" Reality-Way of Adidam Ruchiradam), I also Speak the preliminary listening-practice that is founded upon, and which always intrinsically "Locates", the "Perfect Knowledge" of Truth.

The "Perfect Practice" (Itself) is not dependent on the psycho-physical faculties, or on their functions, or on any conditionally-based and, necessarily, yet ego-based doings of any kind whatsoever. Therefore, the "Perfect Practice" (Itself) cannot be practiced by My beginning devotees. My beginning devotees, in their relative immaturity, cannot possibly practice the "Radical" Reality-Way of Adidam Ruchiradam on

any basis <u>other</u> <u>than</u> the "radical" (or always "at-the-root")
exercise that intrinsically transcends egoity in the context of
its patterning of psycho-physical faculties and functions—
although they <u>can</u> (and, indeed, <u>must</u>) exercise even their
preliminary listening-practice in a truly "radical" (and, thus,
already "at-the-root" and really ego-transcending) manner,
based on devotionally Me-recognizing Communion with Me,
and the thus to-Me-responsive engagement of the preliminary listening-practice of "Perfect Knowledge", and of all of
the other by-Me-Revealed and by-Me-Given practices and
Means. Therefore, the preliminary mode of "Perfect
Knowledge" listening-practice that I Communicate to My formally practicing devotees is, <u>necessarily</u>, <u>only</u> preliminary—
because of the relative immaturity of those who would practice it. The preliminary listening-practice of My "Perfect
Knowledge" Teachings necessarily always involves the exercise of some mode of participatory association with the faculties and functions of the body-mind-complex. Even
though the preliminary listening-practice of My beginning
devotees is entirely a matter of <u>intrinsically</u> transcending the
faculties and functions and "experiential" states of the body-
mind-complex, that practice is (nevertheless) engaged in the
context of a life yet egoically "self"-identified with the faculties and functions and "experiential" states of the body-
mind-complex.

Such is the crucial distinction between <u>preliminary</u> "Perfect
Knowledge" listening-practice and the "Perfect Practice" <u>Itself</u>,
Which is "Perfect Knowledge" practice in Its ultimate (or
Non-conditional, and Intrinsically Non-egoic) form.

2.

By virtue of My Gift of a preliminary form of the practice
of "Perfect Knowledge" to <u>all</u> My formally practicing devotees
who <u>demonstrate</u> and <u>prove</u> right, true, and real devotion to

Me (necessarily, beginning at the foundation adaptation stage of the formal student-beginner practice within the Second Congregation of the only-by-Me Revealed and Given "Radical" Reality-Way of Adidam Ruchiradam), My "Perfect Knowledge" Self-Revelation is enabled to truly become fundamental to the <u>entire</u> practicing culture of Adidam. Rather than being something that is presumed to be "at the end of the line", the (preliminary) "Perfect Knowledge" listening-practice is fundamental throughout the entire course of the formal practice of the total "Radical" Reality-Way of Adidam Ruchiradam, beginning with full adaptation to the Second Congregation student-beginner stage, and until "Perfect Knowledge" becomes a "Perfect Practice".

Indeed, the practice of "Perfect Knowledge" is as fundamental to the total practice of the "Radical" Reality-Way of Adidam Ruchiradam as whole bodily devotional turning to Me—because "Perfect Knowledge" of Me <u>As</u> I <u>Am</u> is the "Root" of the true and right practice of whole bodily devotional turning to Me.

3.

The Only Inherently <u>Perfect</u> Self-Revelation of Truth Is the seventh stage Self-"Bright" Transcendental Spiritual Manifestation of the One and Only and Indivisible and Self-Evidently Divine Conscious Light. Such is the Unique Nature of My Divine Avataric Life and Work. Perfect Truth is <u>Who</u> I <u>Am</u>—and, therefore, It is <u>What</u> I <u>Do</u>.

I am not here on the basis of either conditional tendency or ego. I Stand Apart and Prior—Always and Already. Such is the Perfect Disposition—and the Perfect Position. I (Always Already) Stand Perfectly Prior to the heart-"root". I am apparently Manifested (by Means of Divine Avataric Self-Incarnation) within the conditional "worlds"—but I am always and only to be "Located" <u>As</u> I <u>Am</u>.

Therefore, the preliminary mode of the practice of "Perfect Knowledge" is about "Locating" Me <u>As</u> I <u>Am</u>—by means of the intrinsic transcending of the fault of "objects", and the intrinsic transcending of the fault of "knowledge" and the "known", and the intrinsic transcending of the fault of "subjectivity", and the intrinsic transcending of the fault of "attention" (or "point of view"). Thus, the "Locating" of Me <u>As</u> I <u>Am</u> is inherently and totally coincident with the fundamental practice of whole bodily devotional turning to Me. Then, in due course, when there is the maturity that demonstrates itself as the transcending of the ego-knot (and of all the gross, subtle, and causal dimensions of form and action), the preliminary (and effectively ego-<u>transcending</u>) mode of the practice of "Perfect Knowledge" is out-grown, and replaced by the (ultimate) "Perfect Practice" Itself (or the <u>Inherently</u> Non-conditional and <u>Intrinsically</u> Non-egoic Realization of devotional Communion with Me). When there is the Realization of the non-necessity of all modes of gross, subtle, and causal endeavor or presumption—then, and only then, can the Ultimate True "Perfect Practice" be established (by Means of My Divine Avataric Transcendental Spiritual Grace).

Thus, the preliminary mode of the practice of "Perfect Knowledge" is preliminary precisely <u>because</u> there is not yet the basis for the actual demonstration of the "Perfect Practice" Itself, free of all bondage to (or egoic "self"-identification with) the conditional human apparatus. As long as there is yet such egoic "self"-identification with the conditional human apparatus, there is the <u>preliminary</u> "Perfect Knowledge" listening-practice, and there is a process <u>leading to</u> the fullest true demonstration of the "Perfect Practice" Itself, Beyond (and Prior to) all conditional dependencies.

To engage this preliminary form of the Reality-Way of "Perfect Knowledge"—as soon as you (as My Second Congregation student-beginner devotee) have <u>demonstrated</u> and <u>proven</u> right, true, and real devotion to Me—gives your practice a right orientation and a right perspective of understanding, from the beginning. The only-by-Me Revealed and Given "Radical" Reality-Way of Adidam Ruchiradam is the seventh stage Reality-Way—from the beginning—but you are not, at the beginning, able to practice in the context of the seventh stage of life. However, you can engage a preliminary mode of practice that leads most directly to the "Perfect Practice", if you rightly and consistently exercise the preliminary form of "Perfect Knowledge" listening-practice from the time of your formal sacramental Initiation into that practice.

The practicing culture of Adidam is the seventh stage culture of My Divine Avataric Self-Revelation. The practicing culture of Adidam is not the culture of the first three stages of life, and (then) the fourth stage of life, and (then) the fifth stage of life, and (then) the sixth stage of life—not at all. The practicing culture of Adidam is, from the beginning, about intrinsically and "radically" (or Priorly, and always "at-the-root") transcending all of that—transcending it at the egoic "root" of all of the otherwise would-be (and merely developmental, and always ego-based, and psycho-physically based) stages of life.

If you devotionally recognize Me As My always Self-Revealed State, you are in devotional Communion with Me—As I Am. On that basis, you are always aware of My Intrinsically egoless and Self-Evidently Divine State, and you are always moved to respond to My Avatarically-Born bodily (human) Divine Form of Self-Manifestation—not merely as a conditionally apparent form, but As the Intrinsically egoless Self-Manifestation of My Self-Evidently Divine and Inherently Perfect State. That is the True, Real, and Intrinsic Nature and Process of the "Radical" Reality-Way of Adidam Ruchiradam.

The by-Me-Revealed and by-Me-Given preliminary "Perfect Knowledge" Instructions are not an alternative to the fullest practice of the total by-Me-Revealed and by-Me-Given "Radical" Reality-Way of Adidam Ruchiradam. Rather, My preliminary "Perfect Knowledge" Instructions perfectly coincide with that <u>total</u> process.

I am not the ego's "other". This is Self-Evidently True, if you devotionally recognize Me. Therefore, true and constant devotional recognition of Me (and right devotional relationship to Me) is the basis for the preliminary "Perfect Knowledge" listening-practice (which, in due course, is superseded by the "Perfect Practice" Itself)—and such is also the necessary basis for the <u>total</u> "Radical" Reality-Way of Adidam Ruchiradam as an altogether Perfect Reality-Way.

VI

The Distinction Between
The Preliminary
Listening-Practice
of Perfect Knowledge
and
The Perfect Practice
of Perfect Knowledge

My Teaching-Instruction has always been as It is now: the present-time transcending of egoity itself and of seeking, through devotional recognition-response to Me, devotional turning to Me, and "radical" (or always "at-the-root") "self"-understanding. There is a basic ground of necessary preparation associated with all that must precede the "Perfect Practice"—but the preparatory dimension of the total practice is not, in and of itself, to become forever prolonged, such that what is merely preparatory becomes a separate and never-ending way of life.

From the beginning, My Divine Avataric Reality-Teaching has always been a "Radical" Teaching. I have always referred to My Divine Avataric Reality-Teaching as "Radical"—meaning that It "addresses the 'root' of egoity itself", rather than exploiting and conditionally developing the psycho-physical phenomena associated with the permutations of egoic possibility (gross, subtle, and causal).

Devotional recognition-response to Me is not merely conventional (or nominal) devotionalism. To devotionally recognize Me and devotionally respond to Me is to have come into the Intrinsic Feeling-Apprehension of My Intrinsically egoless and Self-Evidently Divine State. To devotionally recognize Me is to Find Me <u>As</u> My State. To devotionally respond to Me is to turn to Me <u>As</u> My State, and to devotionally Commune with Me through sensitivity to My Avatarically Self-Transmitted Transcendental Spiritual (and Always Blessing) Divine Presence. By Means of simply Sighting Me, one who devotionally recognizes Me and devotionally responds to Me is, thus and thereby, turned to Me by Means of Intrinsic Feeling-Apprehension of My Divine Avataric Self-Transmission of My Intrinsically egoless Self-"Bright" State.

My Divine Avataric Gift to all deals with the "root"-problem of egoity itself, and the entire pattern of "experiencing" and living based on seeking (which pattern develops from that very "root" of "self"-contraction). This is not something that is supposed to take decades—or even your entire life—to figure out. The only-by-Me Revealed and Given "Radical" Reality-Way of Adidam Ruchiradam is not a matter of "interviewing the ego" forever, and (on that basis) merely making piecemeal adjustments in behavior. Rather, the only-by-Me Revealed and Given "Radical" Reality-Way of Adidam Ruchiradam is a "Radical" Teaching, and a "radical" process, founded in "radical" devotion to Me. That "radical" process cuts through the "root" of egoity—and, thus, cuts down the entire "tree" of egoity, at the "root"—even from the beginning of the "Radical" Reality-Way of Adidam Ruchiradam, and by Means of the devotional recognition-response to Me.

Even in the midst of My many Years of Self-Submission to My devotees and the "world", I always Communicated My "Radical" Reality-Teaching—and I always Manifested My Self-"Bright" (seventh stage) State of Realization—in the eyes of everyone. However, the "dialogue" of My Years of Self-Submission is—now, and forever hereafter—ended. My Divine Avataric Self-Submission is Finished and Complete. My Reality-Teaching, in all Its detail, is Fully and Completely Given.

If you devotionally recognize Me and devotionally respond to Me, you are (thereby) moved beyond the patterning of the psycho-physical faculties, to Me—to My Intrinsically egoless and Self-Evidently Divine State, My Self-Evidently Divine Person. Thus, the only-by-Me Revealed and Given "Radical" Reality-Way of Adidam Ruchiradam is "radical"—in the devotional sense—from the beginning.

Devotion to Me is not conventional devotionalism—in the sense of the first three stages of life, or even in the sense of the fourth stage of life. Devotion to Me is "radical" devotion, enacted through devotional recognition-response to Me—turning the four psycho-physical faculties to Me, and ignoring all the contents and patterning of ego-"I".

"Radical" devotion to Me is, itself, the seed of most fundamental "self"-understanding. If such "radical" devotion to Me is the case, most fundamental "self"-understanding will be readily awakened—because "self"-understanding is already established as the circumstance of your practice of the "Radical" Reality-Way of Adidam Ruchiradam, through devotional recognition-response to Me (or persistent devotion to Me, based on devotional recognition of Me).

True devotional recognition of Me is devotional Communion with Me <u>As</u> I <u>Am</u>. Merely to perceive Me as a physical Entity, and to be (thereby) moved to respond to Me in some conventionally devotionalistic sense, is <u>not</u> true devotional recognition of Me. When you truly devotionally recognize Me, your devotional (and, in due course, Transcendental Spiritual) relationship to Me cuts through the "root" of egoity. Such is the "radical" devotional (and, in due course, Transcendental Spiritual) relationship to Me. And, by cutting through the "root" of egoity, the "radical" devotional (and, in due course, Transcendental Spiritual) relationship to Me leads directly (and in due course) to the only-by-Me Revealed and Given "Perfect Practice" of the "Radical" Reality-Way of Adidam Ruchiradam.

Thus, the lifetime of My devotee is not to be a lifetime of "correcting" the ego. Nor is the lifetime of My devotee to be a lifetime of developing the psycho-physical potential of the ego (or the psycho-physically incarnated apparent individual, or apparently separate person). Rather, the lifetime of My devotee is to be a lifetime of <u>transcending</u> the ego.

This "'radical'-from-the-beginning" characteristic of the only-by-Me Revealed and Given "Radical" Reality-Way of Adidam Ruchiradam is given concrete and unambiguous expression by My Divine Avataric Gift of the preliminary "Perfect Knowledge" listening-practice to <u>all</u> My formally practicing devotees who have <u>demonstrated</u> and <u>proven</u> their right, true, and real devotion to Me. This "Radical" Gift

95

of Mine does not eliminate the requirement for devotional turning to Me, or for the exercise of all the by-Me-Given forms of "self"-discipline, or (altogether) for the demonstration of all the by-Me-Given modes of practice of the "Radical" Reality-Way of Adidam Ruchiradam. Rather, the right and true context of your practice of the only-by-Me Revealed and Given "Radical" Reality-Way of Adidam Ruchiradam is your devotional (and, in due course, Transcendental Spiritual) recognition of Me, and your participation in the only-by-Me Revealed and Given "radical" approach to the transcending of egoity. That "radical" approach is (itself) direct—not progressive. Therefore, that "radical" approach is <u>always</u> effective—in the perfect sense—moment to moment. Nevertheless, that "radical" approach requires (and makes possible) a demonstration that matures (by means of the preliminary listening-practice) toward the (eventual) Non-conditional Demonstration of the "Perfect Practice" of the Reality-Way of "Perfect Knowledge".

The preliminary listening-practice of "Perfect Knowledge" is a Teaching That I have Given at the "End-Time" of My Years of Teaching-Submission. That preliminary listening-practice is usable, in the fullest sense, only by those who devotionally recognize Me (<u>As</u> I <u>Am</u>), who are devotionally turned to Me (<u>As</u> I <u>Am</u>), and who (thereby) have the ego under-cut by Communing with Me, moment to moment. Such is the most fundamental secret of practice in My Divine Avataric Company: Practice of the only-by-Me Revealed and Given "Radical" Reality-Way of Adidam Ruchiradam is not a technique, but a <u>relationship</u>. That practice is <u>devotion to Me</u> (<u>As</u> I <u>Am</u>)—necessarily associated with the exercise of the Reality-Way of "Perfect Knowledge" (at first, in a preliminary sense, and, ultimately, in the "Perfect Practice" sense). All other aspects of the only-by-Me Revealed and Given "Radical" Reality-Way of Adidam Ruchiradam are simply the fullness of the practice as it is lived, day by day—such that the entire life (and the whole body) of My devotee is conformed to Me and this "Perfect Knowledge" life.

The preliminary "Perfect Knowledge" listening-practice is not a "something" to be exercised in and of itself (independent of the devotional relationship to Me). My devotees must understand: The preliminary "Perfect Knowledge" listening-practice can be rightly (and fruitfully) exercised only in the context of the (necessarily, formally acknowledged) devotional relationship to Me. Thus, the fundamental characteristics of the only-by-Me Revealed and Given "Radical" Reality-Way of Adidam Ruchiradam are, altogether, the devotional recognition-response to Me, the devotional (whole bodily) turning to Me of the four principal faculties (to the degree of true surrender to Me), the exercise of the by-Me-Given disciplines of right life, and the exercise of the preliminary form of the Reality-Way of "Perfect Knowledge" (until, in due course, that preliminary form becomes the Ultimate, and Non-conditional, "Perfect Practice" of the "Radical" Reality-Way of Adidam Ruchiradam).

The Ultimate, and Non-conditional, "Perfect Practice" of the "Radical" Reality-Way of Adidam Ruchiradam occurs in due course. Until then, the preliminary form of the Reality-Way of "Perfect Knowledge" is to be practiced by all My formally acknowledged Second Congregation devotees, from the time of their formal sacramental Initiation into that practice of the "Radical" Reality-Way of Adidam Ruchiradam— and that preliminary form of the Reality-Way of "Perfect Knowledge" is to be continued, by all My formally acknowledged Second Congregation devotees, and, in due course, by all members of the Forward Lay Congregationist Order of Adidam Ruchiradam and all novice participants in the Lay Renunciate Order of Adidam Ruchiradam and the Ruchira Sannyasin Order of Adidam Ruchiradam, who are, as such, My formally acknowledged First Congregation devotees.

I do not change—but My devotee must go through a process.

Devotion to Me, and the exercise of "Perfect Knowledge"—
that is the only-by-Me Revealed and Given "Radical" Reality-
Way of Adidam Ruchiradam. All other aspects of My
Instruction in the practice of the "Radical" Reality-Way of
Adidam Ruchiradam (including My Instruction in the necessary disciplines of right life) are the necessary elaboration of
the culture of that practice.

The devotional (and, in due course, Transcendental
Spiritual) relationship to Me is Transmitted by virtue of My
Self-Evidently Divine Person, My Self-Evidently Divine State,
and My Self-"Bright" Self-Transmission (Which is Transcen-
dental Spiritual in Nature). My Self-"Bright" Self-Transmission
is What Brings About the Ultimate Fulfillment of the only-by-
Me Revealed and Given Reality-Way of "Perfect Knowledge"—
in the form of the Non-conditional (or "Perfect Practice")
Demonstration of "Perfect Knowledge". Nevertheless, the
only-by-Me Revealed and Given "Radical" Reality-Way of
Adidam Ruchiradam does not become the Reality-Way of
"Perfect Knowledge". Rather, the only-by-Me Revealed and
Given "Radical" Reality-Way of Adidam Ruchiradam Is the
Reality-Way of "Perfect Knowledge" from the beginning—
not as a mere philosophy, or as a mere "self"-applied technique, but as the right and true and real devotional (and, in
due course, Transcendental Spiritual) relationship to Me.

The Reality-Way of "Perfect Knowledge" is not about the
developmental stages of life (in and of themselves). Rather,
the Reality-Way of "Perfect Knowledge" is a Free Way, about
the Free Realization of Reality Itself (Which is Self-Evidently
Divine). Therefore, the Reality-Way of "Perfect Knowledge"
(Which is the only-by-Me Revealed and Given "Radical"
Reality-Way of Adidam Ruchiradam) is an Intrinsically ego-
transcending Way—from Its beginning.

In every moment of true devotional turning to Me, the
practice of the "Radical" Reality-Way of Adidam Ruchiradam
is non-egoic (or Intrinsically ego-transcending, rather than

making egoic psycho-physical structures themselves the means of practice). Therefore, from the beginning, right devotionally Me-recognizing and devotionally to-Me-responding practice of the only-by-Me Revealed and only-by-Me Given "Radical" Reality-Way of Adidam Ruchiradam always intrinsically transcends "self"-contraction, and all bondage to the accumulations (in and as and of the body-mind-"self") that occur as a result of psycho-physical "self"-contraction (or the act of egoity). The true devotional turning to Me goes beyond all of that. Thus, there is the spontaneous unfolding of the signs of the release of ego-bondage during the entire course of preliminary listening-practice (maturing, in due course, into the demonstration that establishes the "Perfect Practice"). Nevertheless, the "experiential" signs of the release of ego-bondage are not themselves the point of the preliminary listening-practice of the "Radical" Reality-Way of Adidam Ruchiradam.

The practice of the only-by-Me Revealed and Given "Radical" Reality-Way of Adidam Ruchiradam is not a matter of doing something to (intentionally, or strategically) "stand back". You are <u>Always</u> <u>Already</u> in the Perfectly Prior Position, in and <u>As</u> Which you engage the right preliminary listening-practice of "Perfect Knowledge". It is not that you must do something to what is "objective", or to what takes the form of the "known", or of "knowledge", or of the "knowing-subject". In the context of its arising, there is the noticing of "object", or of the "known", or of the apparent "knowledge", or of the apparent "knowing-subject"—but <u>you</u> <u>are</u> the "Perfect Knower" (Transcendentally, and Inherently, Free). Therefore, <u>you</u> are <u>never</u> any "known-object" or any mode of the "knowing-subject" in the context of any and all apparent arisings.

Therefore, you do <u>not</u>—if you are rightly exercising the preliminary listening-practice of "Perfect Knowledge"—make any effort or gesture to "stand back" (or to "step back"). In other words, you are not Called by Me to continuously make a gesture that somehow changes the Perfectly Prior Position in and <u>As</u> Which you Always Already Stand. I do <u>not</u> Call or Instruct you to "return" to the Position in Which you Always Already Stand. I simply Call and Instruct you to acknowledge and Abide in the Always Perfectly Prior Position in Which you Always Already Stand.

Thus, moment to moment, simply Stand in the Position you are Always Already in—by clearly "Knowing" (or Intrinsically Self-Comprehending) that you <u>are</u> <u>not</u> in any "position" (or conditional state) <u>other</u> than That.

You are not an "object". You are not anything "known". You are not any kind of "knowing" (or "knowledge"). You are not any mode or kind of a "knowing-subject". You <u>are</u> Always Already in the Position of That Which is <u>not</u> an "object". You <u>are</u> Always Already in the Self-Position of the "Perfect Knower"—but that "Perfect Knower" is <u>not</u> the apparently separate "self" (or ego-"I") that is "functioning-as-knower-through-the-faculties". The merely conditional "knower" is "knowing" the "known"—and is (thus and thereby) identical to the "knowing"-function and the apparent "knowledge". The Transcendental Spiritual "Perfect Knower" is <u>not</u> any of that. The Transcendental Spiritual "Perfect Knower" is <u>not</u> a "known-object" and <u>not</u> a "knowing-subject".

Therefore, the preliminary listening-practice of "Perfect Knowledge" is not merely a philosophical proposition. Rather, the preliminary listening-practice of "Perfect Knowledge" is the Tacit Self-Apprehension (or the Intuitive Self-Apperception), moment to moment, of That Which otherwise seems to take the form of "objects", or the "known", or the "knowledge", or the psycho-physical faculty (or presumed "knowing-self") of the "knowing" of the "knowledge". All of that is "<u>objective</u>". All of that is mere "object"— but the Transcendental Spiritual "Perfect Knower" <u>Is</u> Always Already Perfectly Prior to any and every mode of "known-object" and any and every mode of "knowing-subject".

No "object" is "known", as <u>such</u>, by the Transcendental Spiritual "Perfect Knower". The Transcendental Spiritual "Perfect Knower" <u>Is</u> That Which is always Inherently Self-Indicated by "Transcendental Root-Standing" relative to <u>any</u> "known-object", <u>anything</u> conditionally "known", <u>any</u> conditional "knowing", <u>any</u> mode of conditional "knowledge", and <u>any</u> mode of conditionally "knowing" (and, thus, conditionally existing) "self". "Transcendental Root-Standing" simply Self-Indicates the Transcendental Spiritual "Perfect Knower"—Which <u>Is</u> Always Already Perfectly Prior to <u>all</u> modes of conditionally arising "known-objects" and <u>all</u> modes and operations of a presumed conditionally arising "knowing-self". The Transcendental Spiritual "Perfect Knower" <u>Only</u> and Always Already "Knows" (or Self-Apprehends, or Self-Apperceives) <u>Itself</u> (or the Perfectly Prior and Transcendental Spiritual Self-Nature, Self-Condition, and Self-State <u>Itself</u>)—and <u>all</u> conditionally arising "known-objects" and <u>all</u> modes and operations of a presumed conditionally arising "knowing-self" are, Ultimately (in the context of the "Perfect Practice" of the only-by-Me Revealed and Given seventh stage of life), Divinely Self-Recognized to <u>be</u> merely apparent, non-necessary, and inherently non-binding modifications of the Transcendental Spiritual "Perfect Knower" (or Self-Nature, Self-Condition, and Self-State) <u>Itself</u>.

When you are <u>Priorly</u> (or Always Already) Established in and <u>As</u> That Self-Position Which <u>Is</u> the Transcendental Spiritual "Perfect Knower", <u>It</u> is Non-"objective"—It has <u>no</u> form, It has <u>no</u> mind. It does not "know" <u>conditionally</u>. It does not "know" any conditional "knowledge", or anything otherwise conditionally "known", or any conditionally arising "object" at all. Only That Transcendental Spiritual Self-Position <u>is</u> Truly and Self-Evidently <u>Prior</u>.

The preliminary listening-practice of "Perfect Knowledge" is the Tacit (by-Me-Given) Reality-Way of simply Self-"Locating", moment to moment, the Self-Position in Which you Always Already (or Always Priorly) Stand.

Ultimately, when there is (by Means of My Avatarically Self-Transmitted Divine Transcendental Spiritual Grace) the Perfect Realization of the Self-Position in Which you Always Already Stand, then there is no more practice to be done in relation to the conditional (psycho-physical) apparatus. Then, no preliminary exercise is any longer required to Self-Indicate (or Self-"Locate") That Native Self-Position. You simply <u>Are</u> That—and That Is That. <u>It</u> <u>Is</u> <u>That</u>—and That is the end of it. There is no further preliminary exercise to be done. There is no conditional (psycho-physical) apparatus (whether gross, subtle, or causal) that needs to be used, changed, manipulated, or otherwise gone beyond in any manner (or by any conditionally applied means) whatsoever—because the Perfectly Prior (or Transcendental Spiritual) Self-Position is not merely re-"Located" (or "Found" again) moment to moment, but (rather) It is Priorly (or Intrinsically, and Always Already) Self-Established.

Such is the distinction between the <u>preliminary</u> listening-practice of "Perfect Knowledge" and the (eventual) "<u>Perfect</u> Practice" of "Perfect Knowledge". In the case of the <u>preliminary</u> listening-practice of "Perfect Knowledge", you are always (in effect) re-"Locating" Where you Always Already <u>Are</u>. In the case of the "Perfect Practice" of "Perfect Knowledge", you Always Already <u>Are</u> Where (and <u>As</u>) you Always Already <u>Are</u>. In the context of the "Perfect Practice", Where (or <u>As</u> What) you <u>Are</u> is (simply) Self-Evidently the Case—and, therefore, no further intentional (or conditionally exercised) practice is required to <u>re</u>-"Locate" Where (or <u>As</u> What) you Always Already <u>Are</u>. Such is the Perfect, or Non-conditional, Demonstration of "Perfect Knowledge".

Thus, the only-by-Me Revealed and Given "Perfect Practice" of the "Radical" Reality-Way of Adidam Ruchiradam is not, in and of itself, a matter of the exercise of the "twelve-part process" of "Radical Self-Abiding". "Radical Self-Abiding" is, <u>fundamentally</u> (and <u>Always</u> <u>Already</u>), simply the Self-Comprehending (or Self-Apprehending, or Self-Apperceiving) of the Perfectly Prior (and Transcendental Spiritual) Self-Position (or Self-Nature, Self-Condition, and Self-State) Which has Priorly (and Always Already) been Self-Established. To demonstrate the "Perfect Practice" of "Perfect Knowledge" is simply to persist in That Intrinsic Self-"Locating" of the Self-Position (or Self-Nature, Self-Condition, and Self-State) in and As Which you Always Already Self-Abide. Such is the fundamental demonstration of the three parts of the only-by-Me Revealed and Given "Perfect Practice" of the "Radical" Reality-Way of Adidam Ruchiradam. In the context of the "Perfect Practice" of the "Radical" Reality-Way of Adidam Ruchiradam, the Witness-Position is simply (and Always Already, or Self-Evidently) So—always, and to begin with. Furthermore, in the context of the "Perfect Practice" of the "Radical" Reality-Way of Adidam Ruchiradam, the Witness-Position is (Thus) simply So without any other context or practice required for any kind of confirming (or re-confirming) of It, or Self-Comprehending (or Self-Apprehending) of It, or to establish the Self-Abiding As It. Such is the fundamental process of the only-by-Me Revealed and Given "Perfect Practice" of the "Radical" Reality-Way of Adidam Ruchiradam.

When the "Perfect Practice" becomes fully established As the Tacit Fullness of the Divine Conscious Light (and not merely as the Self-Contained "Subject"-mode of Consciousness-apart-from-"objects")—and, thus, when the "Bright" of My Own Divine Avataric Self-Transmission has entirely undermined all presumption of "otherness" and "difference"—My Transcendental Spiritual Self-Transmission of Self-Radiance is Non-conditionally Self-Apprehended As the Divine Conscious Light, or As Self-Existing and Self-Radiant Consciousness Itself.

Consciousness Itself as the "Subject"-Only—distinguished as That Which is entirely Non-"object", or discerned exclusively, apart from (or somehow dissociated from) "objects"—necessarily feels a tacit sense of "difference". But the Fullest Realization of My "Bright" Transcendental Spiritual Self-Transmission is of such a Nature that all differences are (Ultimately) Intrinsically Transcended, and Perfectly Outshined, in Perfectly Non-exclusive Divine Self-Abiding Self-Recognition of all "objects" (or all apparent differences and even the tacit sense of "difference" itself) As the One and Only and Inherently Indivisible and Intrinsically egoless Divine Conscious Light Itself. There are no differences—and That is the Nature of the only-by-Me Revealed and Given seventh stage Realization.

Consciousness and "objects" are not "different". They are One Indivisible, Self-Existing, Self-Radiant, and Inherently Non-separate (and, Thus, Perfectly egoless) Conscious Light—Utterly and Self-Evidently without "difference". That is the Nature of the only-by-Me Revealed and Given seventh stage Realization.

In the only-by-Me Revealed and Given seventh stage of life, there are no differences.

In the only-by-Me Revealed and Given seventh stage of life, there is not an "object".

In the only-by-Me Revealed and Given seventh stage of life, there is no "not-Self".

In the only-by-Me Revealed and Given seventh stage of life, there is Only the Divine Conscious Light—Which is not "different" from "objects". The "known" and the "knowledge" and the "knowing" are, Ultimately, not "different" from the Transcendental Spiritual "Perfect Knower". However, That is a Perfectly Non-conditional, Transcendental, Inherently Spiritual, Intrinsically egoless, and Self-Evidently Divine Realization.

The characteristic of the Realization associated with the sixth stage of life is that there is a "difference" between the "Subject" and the "object"—even though the "Subject" is of a

Non-conditional (or Transcendental) Nature. This is due to
the nature of the characteristic sixth stage orientation, which,
by means of the exercise of dissociative introversion, strategically turns away from "objects"—by turning back upon
the presumed "knowing-subject". However, the characteristic of the only-by-Me Revealed and Given "Radical" Reality-
Way of Adidam Ruchiradam, from the beginning, and as a
whole, and, therefore, the characteristic of the Perfect
Realization that indicates the only-by-Me Revealed and
Given seventh stage of life, is the characteristic of the
Indivisible Divine Conscious Light, Itself—in Which there is
no dissociative introversion upon any presumed "knowing-
subject" and no presumption of "difference" between
Consciousness and "objects". In That Most Perfect State of
Intrinsically egoless (or Perfectly "subjectless") and Self-
Evidently Divine Self-Realization, all apparent "objects" are,
through My Divine Avataric Transcendental Spiritual Self-
Transmission of the "Bright" (or the Indivisible Conscious
Light) Itself, cancelled in their separateness (or their charac-
teristic of "difference").

The Divine Conscious Light Is One, Indivisible Force,
Which Is Self-Existing and Self-Radiant Consciousness
(Itself). There Is no "difference" between Consciousness and
Light. That is the seventh stage Realization. And That is My
Divine Avataric Self-Revelation, and My Unique Divine
Avataric Self-Manifestation. The Totality of My Divine
Avataric Reality-Teaching corresponds to That, from begin-
ning to end.

Even from Its beginning, the only-by-Me Revealed and
Given "Radical" Reality-Way of Adidam Ruchiradam is not
about the developmental stages of life themselves. Even
from Its beginning, the only-by-Me Revealed and Given
"Radical" Reality-Way of Adidam Ruchiradam is about the
"Perfect Knowledge" That is Awakened by the tacit devotional recognition (and, altogether, whole bodily, or total

psycho-physical, devotional, Transcendental, and, in due course, Spiritual "Locating" and "Knowing") of Me (As I Am). In That devotional Communion with Me, the four psycho-physical faculties are whole-bodily-responsively turned to Me, and the content or patterning of the psycho-physical faculties is (thus and thereby) forgotten in that Non-"objective" Communion with Me As I Am. Thus, "Perfect Knowledge" of Me is Inherent in the right and true devotional recognition-response to Me.

"Perfect Knowledge" is a Divine Transcendental Spiritual Gift, Avatarically Given by Me. "Perfect Knowledge" is not something you "practice" as a kind of philosophical exercise.

Most Perfect Realization of Consciousness Itself Is Love-Bliss Itself. Love-Bliss-Consciousness Itself Is the Divine Transcendental Spiritual Conscious Light—Which Utterly Releases all forms of ego-bondage, and Which (Most Ultimately) Outshines everything.

Therefore, the true "Root"-Practice of "Perfect Knowledge" is not a matter of presuming (in the sixth stage manner) that "self"-conscious "awareness" (or the presumed "knowing-self"), inverted upon itself, and strategically dissociated from its apparent "objects", Is Truth. When I Instruct you in the "Root"-Practice of "Perfect Knowledge", I am not Calling you to invert your attention upon your otherwise everyday "self"-consciousness (or presumed conditional "knowing-self"), and (thus and thereby) to exclude the "objective thingness" of life. The "self"-conscious "awareness" (or presumed "knowing-self", or ego-"I"-presumption) that sits "behind" the perception and cognition of "objects" is not Really existing—and, in any case, it is not, itself (or as a presumed "self"-idea), Love-Bliss. Exclusionary "self"-consciousness is not a Spiritual State.

In My Communication of the Reality-Way of "Perfect Knowledge", I am not suggesting that you should perform an inward-turned act of dissociation from "objects", or that you should strategically disconnect from "things", or that you should treat "objects" and "things" in a kind of xenophobic manner, as if they are "enemy-aliens". Indeed, I must correct all such mistaken notions in My devotees.

The idea that "self"-conscious "awareness", inverted upon itself, and (thus and thereby) strategically dissociated from its perceptual and conceptual "objects", is Most Perfect Divine Self-Realization is an ego-based notion. Only Perfectly egoless Self-Realization of the Intrinsically Transcendental Spiritual Reality—Priorly and Perfectly Self-Existing, Intrinsically Self-Evident, and Non-conditionally Self-Radiant—Is Most Perfect (and Intrinsically egoless) Divine Self-Realization. Most Perfect Divine Self-Realization Is the State of Perfect Love-Bliss-Radiance, the Inherent Radiance of the Self-Existing Reality That Is Conscious Light. It is only when the Spiritual Reality of the Divine Conscious Light is Realized that arising "objects" and the "shadow-self" (or the illusion of an "object"-reflecting "knowing-self", or ego-"I") can be Divinely Self-Recognized.

In the beginning of your practice of the only-by-Me Revealed and Given "Radical" Reality-Way of Adidam Ruchiradam, to engage the preliminary listening-practice of "Perfect Knowledge" is not yet to be Established in Perfect Love-Bliss-Fullness. Such is the distinction between the preliminary listening-practice of "Perfect Knowledge" and the Most Perfect Realization of "Perfect Knowledge": Most Perfect Realization of "Perfect Knowledge" Is the Perfectly Transcendental and Inherently Spiritual Divine Self-Nature, Self-Condition, and Self-State. Most Perfect Realization of "Perfect Knowledge" Is Self-Existing and Self-Radiant—and Absolute.

The preliminary listening-practice of "Perfect Knowledge" is not a practice of inwardly-concentrated inversion upon any "subjective" state or principle of a "knowing-self", or any kind of ego-effort to exclude "objects" from the field of perceptual and conceptual awareness. Rather, the preliminary listening-practice of "Perfect Knowledge" is the practice of Always Already Self-Standing <u>As</u> the Always Already Self-Evident State That <u>Is</u> Always Already Free-Standing Prior to "objects". Thus and So, when the preliminary listening-practice of "Perfect Knowledge" becomes fully and finally Demonstrated <u>As</u> the "Perfect Practice" of "Perfect Knowledge", all-and-All <u>Is</u> Divinely Self-Recognized in and As <u>That</u> Perfectly Prior Self-State—and all-and-All is Outshined in and As <u>That</u> Perfectly Prior Self-State, without excluding the apparent conditionally arising "world" of perceptions, and without any dissociative introversion upon a presumed "knowing-self" (or ego-"I").

The only-by-Me Revealed and only-by-Me Given Means for the Most Perfect Realization of Me are here—now, and forever hereafter. And the only-by-Me Revealed and only-by-Me Given "Radical" Reality-Way of Adidam Ruchiradam is, from beginning to end, about the Divine Self-Nature, Self-Condition, and Self-State Itself (or the Intrinsically egoless Nature, Condition, and State of Reality Itself, or of Truth Itself, or of <u>Real</u> Acausal God).

The conventional idea of "God" as the Great "Other", Who is the "Maker" of things, and of separate egos, and so forth, is a concept of ordinary (or exoteric) "religiosity"—an idea that comes from the ego-position of "self"-contracted identification with the body-mind-"self". From the standpoint of that conventional concept of "Creator-God", there is already "a body in a cosmos"—and you are seeking to account for why the <u>body</u> is there. That is where the conventional "Creator-God" myth comes from. However, if you <u>are</u> in the Reality-Position, all of what conditionally arises has a totally Transcendental Spiritual context of significance—and All of all-and-All is Comprehended (or, rather, Self-Apprehended) in an Utterly Non-differentiated Manner. That is the Ultimate Matter of Reality and Truth—or of <u>Real</u> (Acausal) God.

The only-by-Me Revealed and Given seventh stage
Reality-Way is on the "Other Side" of (or Perfectly Prior to)
egoity—whereas all conventional "religiosity" is "made" on
"this side" of egoity, or from the position (or "point of
view") of egoity itself, and, thus, from the position (or "point
of view") of separateness, and of the "world" as a "something" which already exists, and which you account for
through devotionalistic feeling and philosophical notions
about the "Divine Nature" of "things". But all of that is
merely imaginative speculation, based on an ego-"I", sitting
in a conditionally apparent "room"—rather than transcending
the categories of the apparently separate person, the apparent
"objectivity" of the "world", the apparent "knowledge" of it,
and the futile ego-effort to figure out how "this" is (somehow)
coming from (or being "caused" by) an "Ultimate Source"
That is Beyond all conditions.

The Perfect Reality-Way must Always Already Stand
Beyond and Prior to the position (or "point of view") of the
separate entity in a conditionally apparent "room".

The True (and Truly Perfect) "First Room", then, is simply
the "Place" of Ultimate (or Perfect) "Consideration", the
"Place" of the Ultimate "Brightness" of the Perfect Self-
Realization of Reality Itself. The True (and Inherently
Perfect) "First Room" is the Self-Existing and Self-Radiant
"Room" That Is Reality Itself—and the Self-Existing and Self-
Radiant "Room" That Is Reality Itself is Inherently without
"difference". The Inherently Perfect "First Room" is Non-
conditional and Indivisible. The Inherently Perfect "First
Room" Is Self-"Bright" (or Self-Existing and Self-Radiant)
Conscious Light.

Right practice of the only-by-Me Revealed and only-by-Me
Given "Radical" Reality-Way of Adidam Ruchiradam Always
Already and Intrinsically Transcends all of the developmen-
tal stages of life. It Always Already and Intrinsically
Transcends all ordinariness of egoic living. It Always Already

and Intrinsically Transcends all conventional "religiosity", and all the conventional and ego-based ideas of "Reality", and of "God", and so forth, that come with the "all" of ego-"I".

Right practice of the only-by-Me Revealed and only-by-Me Given "Radical" Reality-Way of Adidam Ruchiradam Always Already and Intrinsically Transcends all conventional esotericism of a Spiritual Nature, and all "Ultimate Exercises" of a psycho-physical kind which have been used as means to seek Realization and Enlightenment by countless people, for all of human time.

Right practice of the only-by-Me Revealed and only-by-Me Given "Radical" Reality-Way of Adidam Ruchiradam Always Already and Intrinsically Transcends all seeking for Reality, Truth, and "God".

My Divine Avataric Self-Revelation is the Self-Revelation of Reality Itself—Which is Self-Evidently Divine and Indivisible.

I Am That. I am not merely communicating a philosophy about That.

I Am the Means for the Most Perfect Divine Self-Realization of Reality.

I Am the Perfect Realization, and I Am the Way of the Perfect Realization, and I Give the Perfect Teaching of That Perfect Realization.

My Fundamental Reality-Teaching is the "Radical" Communication of "Perfect Knowledge" and of the "Radical" Reality-Way of the true and perfect devotional recognition of Me.

The Reality-Way That I Avatarically Reveal and Give is the Divine Reality-Way of the "Bright"—Which Is My Divine Avataric Self-Manifestation, from Birth, and Always Already Perfectly Prior to Birth, and Always Already now, and, therefore, always forever hereafter, even forever after My Divine Avataric physical human Lifetime.

Therefore, I have always Said—and It Is So—that I must
be devotionally recognized, As I Am. I must be devotionally
recognized—if the devotional relationship to Me is to be
fruitful as the Awakening of My any and each and every
devotee to the actual right "Perfect Knowledge" practice of
the "Radical" Reality-Way of Adidam Ruchiradam, and, in
due course, to Most Perfect Divine Self-Realization.

My true devotees do not merely attain to Me eventually.
My true devotees begin with Me. And the entire "Radical"
Reality-Way of Adidam Ruchiradam Is with Me—in My
"House".

In the course of the only-by-Me Revealed and Given
devotional practice of Abiding with Me in My "First Room",
My true devotee (in the always "radical", or "at-the-root",
context of practice-demonstration) out-grows all the possible
kinds of phenomenal associations—but My true devotee is
always (even Perfectly) with Me the entire time.

My true devotee's ego-transcending devotional Communion with Me intrinsically transcends all that may apparently
happen—or merely seem to happen—in the conditionally
apparent "world"-and-lifetime that appears to arise in the
conditionally arising "Happening" that appears in apparent
association with the Perfect Context and Domain of the
"First Room" of Me.

VII

The Imposition of Pattern

T he preliminary "Perfect Knowledge" listening-practice is to be integrated, on a day to day basis, with all the other by-Me-Given (functional, practical, relational, and cultural) modes of practice of the "Radical" Reality-Way of Adidam Ruchiradam—including all the by-Me-Given disciplines of right life and of whole bodily devotional Invocation of Me. Indeed, all aspects and requirements of the by-Me-Given disciplines of right life and of whole bodily devotional Invocation of Me must be regularly practiced and intact in the context of daily life if My any formally practicing First or Second Congregation devotee is to be invited to participate in full formal retreats. Therefore, during any period of formal retreat (of either First Congregation or Second Congregation practice in the "Radical" Reality-Way of Adidam Ruchiradam), My devotee must focus intensively, moment to moment, on the exercise of whole bodily devotional turning to Me and the "Perfect Knowledge" listening-practice.

When My devotee makes the formal transition to the intensive listening-hearing stage of the "Radical" Reality-Way of Adidam Ruchiradam, devotion to Me is (necessarily) already being demonstrated as the moment to moment searchless (or whole bodily surrendering and, thus and thereby, actively ego-transcending) Beholding of Me. Nevertheless, the searchless Beholding of Me is still the fundamental devotional practice of whole bodily turning to Me. When that fundamental devotional practice has reached the point of a certain maturity, then it can be described as the searchless Beholding of Me. When My devotee is searchlessly Beholding Me, then the preliminary "Perfect Knowledge" listening-practice can become even more firmly established, with the searchless Beholding of Me as its "root"-basis.

When My searchlessly Me-Beholding devotee is (formally) Transcendentally Spiritually Initiated by Me, My Transcendental Spiritual Transmission of My Inherently Perfect Divine State is felt—and My devotee's "Locating" and

"Knowing" of My Transcendental Spiritual Self-Transmission then becomes the Means for the preliminary "Perfect Knowledge" listening-practice to become even yet more profound and full—such that, in due course, the Transcendental Spiritual Evidence of the searchlessly Me-Beholding preliminary "Perfect Knowledge" listening-practice is shown in the Mode of the "Thumbs", Which is My Divine Transcendental Spiritual Gift That Draws My devotee into the "Perfect Practice" of "Perfect Knowledge".

The "Perfect Practice" is a State—not an activity. My Transcendental Spiritual Self-Transmission is the Transmission of My Self-Evidently Divine State. My Transcendental Spiritual Self-Transmission Establishes the "Perfect Practice". I Am That (literal) Transmission. My Transcendental Spiritual Self-Transmission is "Located" and "Known" whole bodily, As the "Thumbs". Thus, the "Thumbs" Establishes the State That Is the "Perfect Practice". In Truth, I Establish the "Perfect Practice"—because I Am the State That Is the "Perfect Practice", and I Establish That State (of the "Perfect Practice") by Means of the "Thumbs".

The "Thumbs" Is the "Bright"—Self-Manifested As Transcendental Spiritual Self-Transmission. The "Perfect Practice" is the practice of the "Bright" That is Established by Means of My Divine Avataric Transcendental Spiritual Self-Transmission of the "Thumbs"—Which Is the Transcendental Spiritual Self-Manifestation of the Divine Self-Nature, Self-Condition, and Self-State (or the "Bright" Itself, or the One and Indivisible Divine Conscious Light).

The State That Is the "Perfect Practice" is not accomplished through a process of mere thinking. The State That Is the "Perfect Practice" is (necessarily) Transcendentally Spiritually Established. The "Thumbs" Establishes the State of the "Bright". Thus, the Awakening to the "Perfect Practice" is accomplished by Transcendental Spiritual Means. The Awakening to the "Perfect Practice" is not the result of any form of thinking about My preliminary "Perfect Knowledge" Teachings and My "Perfect Practice" Teachings. My "Perfect Practice" Teachings Speak to a State That has been Transcendentally Spiritually Established (by Means of My Avatarically Self-Transmitted Divine Transcendental Spiritual Grace). Therefore, My "Perfect Practice" Teachings are not reducible to any kind of instruction on any yet to be "self"-applied "method" (or seeker's technique) of how to achieve That State.

Transcendental Spiritual participation in My Self-Evidently Divine State is true devotion to Me—and Transcendental Spiritual participation in My Self-Evidently Divine State is the only-by-Me Revealed and Given "Radical" Reality-Way of Adidam Ruchiradam

Thus, the only-by-Me Revealed and Given "Radical" Reality-Way of Adidam Ruchiradam is the Intrinsic Transcendental (and Inherently Spiritual) Self-Manifestation of the Divine Self-Nature, Self-Condition, and Self-State—and My true devotee participates in That Divine Self-Manifestation by participating in devotional Communion with Me, Wherein the Divine Self-Nature, Self-Condition, and Self-State is Transcendentally Spiritually Self-Manifested, and (Thus and Thereby) Self-Revealed As Is.

Devotion to Me is the context in which the Realization of the Divine Self-Nature, Self-Condition, and Self-State is Revealed. Words do not Reveal That Realization. Yes, words are in the Domain of My Person and of Realization of Me (Who Am the State That Is)—but the Means of Realization is Transcendental Spiritual.

In order to approach Me rightly, you must be rightly prepared. You must be established in whole bodily devotional turning to Me, and (thus and thereby) surrendered (whole bodily) to Me. You must tacitly "Know" Who I Am, and tacitly "Know" how to be sensitive to Me and how to "Locate" Me Transcendentally Spiritually. You must tacitly "Know" how to rightly participate in My House, in My Person, in My

State. You must never ignore My Transcendental Spiritual Transmission of My Divine State. And you must not "filter" My Transcendental Spiritual Transmission of My Divine State through your own exercise of "self"-contraction, thereby "experiencing" Me only in secondary (or merely conditional "experiential", or merely psycho-physical) terms. Do not merely let My Transcendental Spiritual Force Fill your little room. Rather, come to My House, and enter My Room, free of "self"-contraction.

If you come into My most immediate Sphere without the necessary preparation, then you become deluded by your own pattern's manipulation of My Self-Radiant Field of Transcendental Spiritual Presence. Indeed, the ego-patterned manipulation of the Divine Self-"Brightness" is the source of the first six stages of life. The first six stages of life are what eventuates when the structures of the body-mind-complex intervene to pattern the Force of the Divine Self-Nature, Self-Condition, and Self-State. Only when all such ego-patterning is transcended is there direct Communion (and "Root"-Identification) with the Divine Self-Nature, Self-Condition, and Self-State and the Transcendental Spiritual Self-Reality.

The first six stages of life are not the means of Most Perfect Divine Self-Realization. The first six stages of life are not the circumstance of Most Perfect Divine Self-Realization. The first six stages of life are a pattern of conditional (or psycho-physical) seeking that imposes itself on the (Intrinsic) Transcendental Spiritual Self-Manifestation of Reality Itself. Thus, when a person says to Me, "I am having visions, I am Spiritually Aware of You," that is merely the body-mind-"self" making visions out of Me.

Therefore, the "root"-gift that must be brought to Me by My devotees is the condition of moment to moment intrinsic transcending of the patterns of "self"-contraction. When that gift is brought, then My devotee is simply, Intrinsically, and Non-conditionally Aware of Me—and, Thus and Thereby, prepared to rightly approach Me, and able to participate in

My Divine Avataric Transcendental Spiritual Company. Then My Divine Avataric Transcendental Spiritual Self-Transmission Works Intrinsically to Awaken the "Perfect Practice".

However, if My devotee is still wrapped up in the "self"-contracted modes of human existence, those "self"-contracted modes—even if they are subtle or causal in nature, rather than merely gross—will inevitably pattern how My devotee "experiences" My Avatarically Self-Transmitted Divine Transcendental Spiritual Presence. The only-by-Me Revealed and Given "Radical" Reality-Way of Adidam Ruchiradam is not about the "great path of return" (via the first six stages of life). The only-by-Me Revealed and Given "Radical" Reality-Way of Adidam Ruchiradam is about directly entering into (and being Priorly Established in) My House, My Domain—by Means of an ego-transcending approach to Me. When you have truly entered into My House, the first six stages of life have become non-necessary and obsolete.

The only-by-Me Revealed and Given "Radical" Reality-Way of Adidam Ruchiradam is not about the first six (or conditional, or ego-based) stages of life. Rather, the only-by-Me Revealed and Given "Radical" Reality-Way of Adidam Ruchiradam is about the seventh stage of life, or Most Perfect Divine Self-Realization (or Intrinsic Realization) of Reality Itself. The transcending of egoity is the transcending of the first six stages of life—intrinsically, at the "root".

Whatever is present in the pattern of the body-mind-complex, or anything and all that would modify My Avatarically Self-Transmitted Divine Transcendental Spiritual Presence into the various "experiential" forms characteristic of the first six stages of life, should, moment to moment, be immediately understood as such. In every moment of right practice of the only-by-Me Revealed and Given "Radical" Reality-Way of Adidam Ruchiradam, My devotee must go beyond all conditional (or psycho-physical) "experiences", rather than seek them, or otherwise cling to them, as if they were (themselves) the Divine Self-Revelation. Instead of clinging to such "experiences", you must understand them to be an imposition of the ego-pattern—a kind of mirrored (or reflected) sign, rather than the Sign of the Mirror (or the Perfectly Prior Reflecting-Witness) Itself (Which is Always Already without patterning).

Therefore, when phenomena of a conditional kind arise in the case of My devotees who are Transcendentally Spiritually Communing with Me, My such devotees go beyond those phenomena simply by means of the exercise of "radical" (or always "at-the-root") devotion to Me (or whole bodily searchless Beholding of Me) and participation in the (at first, preliminary, and, in due course "Perfect") practice of "Perfect Knowledge". The ego-transcending practice of the "Radical" Reality-Way of Adidam Ruchiradam always goes beyond patterned phenomena of a conditional (or psycho-physical) kind. Right practice of the only-by-Me Revealed and Given "Radical" Reality-Way of Adidam Ruchiradam always transcends the ego-patterning of the first six stages of life.

When there is no more patterning to transcend in order to Realize the Perfect Position (or the Divine Self-Nature, Self-Condition, and Self-State Itself), then "Practice" of the only-by-Me Revealed and Given "Radical" Reality-Way of Adidam Ruchiradam has become Most Perfect (or Really of the only-by-Me Revealed and Given seventh stage of life). The Perfect Position Is the Position in Which all phenomena are (Inherently) Divinely Self-Recognizable—and, therefore, no longer binding, and no longer (in any sense) necessary. In the Perfect Position, all arising phenomena are Divinely Self-Recognized to be merely apparent modifications of the Divine Self-Nature, Self-Condition, and Self-State, Infused with the "Brightness" of the Divine Self-Nature, Self-Condition, and Self-State—Ultimately, to the degree of Perfect Outshining.

Such is the Process in My Divine Avataric Transcendental Spiritual Company.

VIII

The Mirror
and
The Checkerboard

1.

A s the ego-"I", you function as the body does with reference to Consciousness Itself—in ignorance of the Consciousness-Position. It is as if the cells of the physical body "meet" together in order to determine how they are going to "dictate"—in an entirely insubordinate manner—the pattern of existence for Consciousness Itself! Then, Consciousness, without direct and intuitive understanding of Its Own Condition, "goes along" with these "demands"—as if the body <u>were</u>, in fact, the Identity of Consciousness Itself. Such is the essence of egoity.

For Consciousness to Wake Up to Its Own Self-Position (or to Recognize Its Own State) <u>is</u> Divine Self-Realization. However, Divine Self-Realization is not merely a mental process. Rather, Divine Self-Realization is, necessarily, a <u>Transcendental</u> <u>Spiritual</u> process. And the Real Transcendental Spiritual process requires the orientation of devotion—which is the orientation to What <u>Is</u> Beyond the "self"-knot. To embrace the life of devotion to Me, My devotee must cease to "grant" the body (or the total body-mind-complex, or the complex psycho-physical totality) the "right" to "design" the pattern of his or her existence.

In Reality, the body is <u>not</u> senior to Consciousness Itself. In Reality, Consciousness Itself is Senior—subordinate to nothing and no one.

However, in the human "world", everything is patterned by ego. Once the ego-pattern "gets rolling", it replicates itself automatically. For that pattern to be corrected, you <u>must</u> become aware of what you (as ego) are doing, and you <u>must</u> change your act—and you <u>must</u> be culturally <u>obliged</u>, by means of systematic accountability, to change your act (based on right "self"-observation and right "self"-understanding). All of this is <u>required</u> in order for the Transcendental Spiritual process to be Real—and It <u>cannot</u> be otherwise.

Without My Divine Avataric Intrusion into your life, your ego-pattern merely replicates itself endlessly, relative to everything whatsoever—and you remain trapped in the ego-possessed domain of "point of view". The ego-patterning of each individual human being, and even the collective ego-patterning of humanity as a whole, is ceaselessly replicated—very much in the manner of cellular reproduction.

The fundamental by-Me-Revealed and by-Me-Given Law of true Spiritual life (and even of true human life) is this: Never subordinate the Source. If that fundamental Law is discarded, there is not anything that is right. As soon as that one Law is cancelled, the ego-pattern starts taking over everything, in the manner of cellular reproduction. The ego manifests itself virtually infinitely, in a checkerboard pattern that replicates its own state and position.

As soon as there is the ego-position (or "self"-contraction), there is the entire conditionally manifested universe. When there is no "self"-contraction, there is no conditionally manifested universe.

You are "Narcissus". You are looking at an image, and you think the image is actually "there"—as something outside you, as something that has nothing to do with you, except that you are seeing it as an "object". As "Narcissus", you are controlled by that "known-object". You have already taken up the ego-position—and, from that position, you even regard Me as a "known-object", "digitalizing" Me into the checkerboard that extends from your little block of presumption.

In the ancient Greek myth, Narcissus is absorbed in an image—but he does not even notice that it is an image in a mirror. The key to understanding "Narcissus" (or the ego-"I") is not that the "self"-image is an image of oneself. Rather, the key to understanding "Narcissus" (or the ego-"I") is that the "self"-image is an image reflected in and by a mirror.

The entire "world" of apparently "objective" reality is a mirrored (or reflected) thing. What is its Source? What is its Source-Condition, or "Root"-Condition?

The Mirror (or Consciousness Itself) Is the Source (or the Perfectly Prior and all-and-All-Reflecting Self-Nature, Self-Condition, and Self-State) of all-and-All.

What Is the State of the Mirror? What Is the Mirror?

The Mirror Is the Truth. The Mirror Is Reality Itself. The Mirror Is Me—the Self-Existing and Self-Radiant Self-Nature, Self-Condition, and Self-State of Reality Itself.

The Mirror Is the Truth. The reflected imagery of "self" and "world" is not the Truth. The State of the Mirror Itself Is the Truth. The "objects" seen in the Mirror are not the Truth.

However, merely to hear this Statement of Mine is not sufficient. The ego may be satisfied with merely hearing My Words—but, in order for the Truth of What I am Saying to actually be Realized, you must change your act, and change your entire life.

Therefore, My devotee must always live in right relationship to Me—subordinating ego-"I" to Me, living by My Divine Avataric Word and Person, entering into devotional Communion with Me, and (thus and thereby) entering into the Position That Is Perfectly Prior to "point of view".

I am not looking in a mirror. I Am the Mirror, or the Water Itself—all the while. As "Narcissus", you do not accept that I Am the Mirror. As "Narcissus", you presume that what you see in the Mirror is you—and that I am merely some kind of metaphor, representing something that is really about you. No—the Mirror does not represent anything. You are the representation (or re-presentation). You are the reflected "object".

I Am Always Already Present, Directly Before you, As the Mirror—but you, as "Narcissus", merely persist in looking at the image of yourself, and either admiring the image or recoiling from it (depending on your attitude of the moment). In either case, you remain in the position of looking at a reflection.

Real practice of the only-by-Me Revealed and Given "Radical" Reality-Way of Adidam Ruchiradam is exactly the opposite of the "Narcissus"-position. Looking at the reflection is not the practice I have Revealed and Given. Looking at the reflection is egoity. Looking at the "object", looking at separate "self", analyzing your "case", living the repetitions of your ego-patterning day to day to day to day, until death—all of that is mummery. That is the reflection-game. That is bondage.

Everyone is involved in a primary "cult of pairs"—the "relationship" to "self", the "relationship" between the ego-"I" and "its" reflection. That is the primary "relationship" for everyone: Always staring at your own reflection, in the form of an illusory ego-"I" (or "knowing-self").

If you are simply bodily present, you do not have a shape. In order to see yourself as a shape, you have to abstract yourself from your own Intrinsic Position, because you have to see yourself reflected from outside. In other words, you have to look in a mirror—either a literal mirror or (otherwise) the mirror of perceptual processes and social associations that give you a sense of outline, a sense of space and time, and so forth.

"Consider" this: Every perception takes time. Therefore, remarkably, you are never in the present moment, with reference to conditional appearances. You are always "afterwards"—because it takes a fraction of a second for any perception to register in the brain. Therefore, none of your phenomenal "experiencing" is in present time. All phenomenal "experience" is mirrored—and you are constantly occupied with your mirrored (or reflected) existence.

The only-by-Me Revealed and Given Reality-Way of "Perfect Knowledge" (Which is the "Radical" Reality-Way of the Heart, or the "Radical" Reality-Way of Adidam Ruchiradam) is not about your mirrored (or reflected) existence. The Reality-Way of "Perfect Knowledge" is not even about the "I"-thought at the core of your presumed separate "selfhood"—because even the "I"-thought is simply another mode of mirroring (or reflection).

The only-by-Me Revealed and Given Reality-Way of "Perfect Knowledge" is <u>solely</u> about the State That <u>Is</u> Truth (<u>Itself</u>), or Reality (<u>Itself</u>)—Perfectly Prior to reflections, Perfectly Prior to "objectification". That State need not be "achieved"—because It Is Always Already The Case. Such is your Real Situation—Perfectly Prior to "point of view", Perfectly Prior to "known-object", Perfectly Prior to conditional "knowledge", Perfectly Prior to reflection, Perfectly Prior to the entire game and mummery and tragedy of "Narcissus". Reality Itself, That Which Is Always Already The Case, Is Perfectly Prior to <u>any</u> and <u>every</u> problem. Therefore, there is <u>never</u> any problem-"object" to be presumed as the basis for a "program" of seeking for Realization of Reality Itself.

All practice-responsibilities in the "Radical" Reality-Way of Adidam Ruchiradam are subordinate to the primary matter of the Intrinsic Self-Realization of Reality Itself. The Intrinsic (or Self-Intuitive) "Knowledge" of Reality Itself is the case in every instant of devotional recognition-response to Me. And that Self-Intuitive "Knowledge" is the case in every moment of "Perfect Knowledge" practice. Thus, the practice of whole bodily devotional turning to Me <u>and</u> "Perfect Knowledge" is the twofold "Root"-Practice of the only-by-Me Revealed and Given "Radical" Reality-Way of Adidam Ruchiradam. All the by-Me-Given disciplines of right life extend from This Reality-"Root" (or "Radical" devotional "Knowledge") That is Priorly Free. The Purpose (or Reality-Significance) of the by-Me-Given disciplines of right life is to enable (or to really demonstrate) the Perfectly Prior Disposition That is Inherently Free, such that the Priorly Free Disposition may Self-Manifest in the midst of the conditions of existence. And, indeed, if you do not fully embrace and truly live the by-Me-Given disciplines of right life, you are (in that case) always assuming the reflected (or mirrored) position, in which "known-objects" and "shadow-self" (or "object-subject" reflections) appear to be senior to the Intrinsically Self-Evident (and Perfectly Subjective, or Intrinsically egoless and Self-Evidently Divine) Self-Nature, Self-Condition, and Self-State of Reality Itself.

To devotionally recognize Me is not to be familiar with Me as an "objective other". Rather, to devotionally recognize Me is to "Locate" My Self-Evidently Divine State, to be moved to Me through devotional recognition of My Self-Evidently Divine State. All other modes of familiarity with Me are modes of "objectification". No mode of "objectification" is devotional recognition of Me. Devotional recognition of Me is not merely to "objectively know" what My bodily (human) Form looks like. True devotion to Me is a matter of "Locating" Me As I Am. True devotion to Me is to tacitly "Know" My Self-Evidently Divine State, all the faculties turned to Me As I Am. And that whole bodily turning to Me As I Am is also true of the preliminary "Perfect Knowledge" listening-practice—because that "Root"-Practice is the moment to moment re-assertion of the Intrinsically Self-Evident State of Reality Itself, Which Is the Communion-with-Me State.

As "Narcissus", you do not accept the practice I have Revealed and Given to you. Therefore, as "Narcissus", you persistently tend to "objectify" Me and impose your own ego-patterning on Me and (thus) to "keep your distance". As "Narcissus", you remain fascinated by a little reflection on the Mirror surface.

I Am here, Spontaneously (Avatarically and Divinely) Appeared. And, just as you do what you do by tendency, I Do What I Do In Truth—As Reality Itself—Self-Manifested in this conditional realm, and Utterly Free of "point-of-view" bondage.

In Appearing here, I am surrounded by the checker-board—shifted around in this maze of squares, of stops, of limits in time and space. Repetition, appearance, shift, change. Shift, shift, shift—but always the same. That time-and-space domain of klik-klak is (itself) conditional, with all kinds of limitations. Nevertheless, time-and-space is a domain in which, paradoxically, My Free Divine Avataric Appearance can be Self-Manifested.

The appearance of an ordinary checkerboard is very orderly—suggesting that everything is in order, and (thus) "all right". All such apparent order is a symmetry based on repetitions. However, the seeming order of the checkerboard is not Truth. The seeming order of the checkerboard is not the Condition of Reality Itself. Rather, the seeming order of the checkerboard is an "object"-imposition, a reflection. The checkerboard seems to be orderly because it is generated from a single square which multiplies itself—in principle, infinitely. The result of that replication-process is a vast checkerboard that appears to be strictly organized.

Such is a metaphor for the usual presumption about the nature of the conditionally manifested universe. According to the conventions of human language and human thinking, the universe is "one thing", which is organized in every detail—and which is "given" to human beings for the paradisiacal purpose of their own "self"-fulfillment. All such thinking is nonsense—an utter fabrication, with no basis whatsoever in Reality. If the universe is so orderly, why does everybody die? Why is everyone subject to so much suffering? Why is this mode of existence characterized by suffering? It is not merely that bad "experience" is potential here. This orderly universe is suffering. The checkerboard is suffering. It is not merely a matter of how any particular game of checkers works out. No—the checkerboard (in and of itself) is limitation, confinement, non-Reality, bondage, stress, search, and mortality. The checkerboard—in and of itself—is intolerable.

You are supposed to notice this! You are supposed to notice—with every breath, every morning, every day—that this orderly universe, in and of itself, is hell! This, in and of itself, is <u>bondage</u>. The checkerboard does not have good intentions—and neither does it have bad intentions. The checkerboard has <u>no</u> intentions. The checkerboard is simply a pattern replicating, generating seed-forms that are totally arbitrary, non-necessary, and merely apparent modifications of the all-and-All-Reflecting (or Acausal) Condition That <u>Is</u> Reality Itself.

Reality Itself <u>Is</u> Freedom. Reality Itself <u>Is</u> Divinity. Reality Itself <u>Is</u> the Only Real (Acausal) God. Reality Itself is not the checkerboard, not the digital field of cosmic "Nature", not the perceived universe, not the mind, not anything "objecti-fied", not any form of conditional "knowledge". Reality Itself Is That Which Is Always Already Perfectly Prior—Perfectly Prior to conditional "knowledge", Perfectly Prior to "known-object". Reality Itself Is the Divine Self-Nature, Self-Condition, and Self-State That <u>Is</u> the Source-Condition of all-and-All—no matter what apparently arises.

That <u>Is</u> the Truth. That <u>Is</u> Reality Itself. That <u>Is</u> Perfectly Self-Sufficient, lacking no thing whatsoever. This must be Realized. That Realization is what makes the Earth-"world" (or conditional life) <u>not</u> hell—even in the midst of all appar-ent arising.

Godless universe is hell. Godless and Guruless "every day" is hell. Humanity is constantly pronouncing the advo-cacy of hell—as if hell were your choice, as if hell were entirely "swell". It is <u>not</u>! This "world" is seeded with death. This "world" is ignorance. This "world" always does not yet "Know" Reality Itself. This "world" is, as such, Godless. This "world", in and of itself, is suffering. Nevertheless, human beings are all advocating this "world" simply because, here and there, you have your miscellaneous little pleasures of this and that. Therefore—because you have your pleasures, because you have this checkerboard that looks so orderly, and because your seeking can entirely occupy you—you conclude that your ego-position in this "world" is to be defended at all costs. You are all ignorantly defending your separate position (or "point of view" in space-time) within the comprehensive mummery of egoic life. In that disposition, you inevitably subordinate Me to your presumed "self", and to the pattern that you think is Reality—whereas, in Reality, that pattern is nothing but mummery. That pattern (including its "shadow-self") is a reflected "object"—always "after the fact" of Reality Itself, always "post-Reality".

What Is Reality? What Is the Reality-Condition, moment to moment? That Is What there is to Realize—not endless talk about the "known-object", the reflection, the "shadow", the ego-"I".

The fundamental uniqueness, the essential characteristic, and the Inherent Truth of the "Radical" Reality-Way of Adidam Ruchiradam is that Reality Itself is "out front"—from the beginning, moment to moment.

2.

I have Visited the "tower room" where klik-klak is happening. I am Telling you that is what is happening. It is dreadful. It is hell. Klik-klak, klik-klak—shift, shift, shift. In and of itself, it is dark, and deadly—and you are caught in it, as if drifting along in some giant intestine, waiting to be crapped out.

In the meantime, what are you doing? You are "hanging out" in that dark "shit-pipe". That is all you are doing here—because you will not accept the Prior Principle That Is Reality Itself. You will not bend the knee—and subordinate separate "self" (or the presumed "shadow-self", or "knowing-self") to What is Perfectly Great.

The klik-klak checkerboard is the actual nature of the conditional apparition of the all-and-All-Reflecting Reality. When you get up close, then you can see the checkerboard, the field of repetition, the field of appearance-shift-change.

133

The black and white squares of the checkerboard just shift into different patterns, making pictures. When you stand far back, you see the pictures, but when you get up close, all there is is the "checkerboard" (or the "grid", as I have also called it). There is a grid in the Energy-Field That Is Consciousness Itself—and all of this appearance of universe is merely bits on that grid. In and of itself, the grid is a terrible illusion, a mere reflection.

The question is not "What is being reflected?" The question is "What is reflecting it?", or "What is the Condition in Which the reflected image is appearing?"

The Mirror Is Reality Itself, Which is Acausal. The Mirror does not "cause" what appears reflected on Its surface. The Mirror Is Perfectly Prior to what appears reflected on Its surface. The Mirror does not change what is reflected on Its surface, and It does not "causatively" originate what is reflected on Its surface.

Whatever is "causative" is inherently conditional. Reality Itself Is, paradoxically, Acausal—not "causing" anything. Reality Itself Is the Source—in the sense that whatever arises is merely an apparent modification of Reality Itself—but Reality Itself does not make anything happen. Reality Itself does not insist. Therefore, none of what arises has any ultimate necessity. None of what arises is Reality Itself. Rather, what arises is merely an appearance based on the (merely apparent) modification of Reality Itself.

When you see What is being played on, when you Self-"Locate" the Mirror—the Self-State of That Which is Acausal and Merely Reflecting, relative to Which nothing arising has any ultimate necessity, nothing arising has any binding force—then you have become Established in the Perfectly Prior Position. The Perfectly Prior Position is not "you". The Perfectly Prior Position is not the nature of the egoic "self"—and, in Truth, there is no egoic "self". The Perfectly Prior Position is Acausal—meaning there is no separate "anyone" there. That is not a state to be achieved. That Is the State That Is Always Already The Case—not the separate "point of view" on the checkerboard, not the presumed independent entity, not the checkerboard-field of universe.

In Reality, ego is not at the "Root" of the "world", not at the "Root" of the body. In Reality, the body is a reflection. Therefore, to think of the ego-"self" as the body is to think of Reality as a "known-object". What about the "Subject"-Position That Is Perfectly Prior to the reflection? Before you look in the Mirror, What Is the Case? What Is Always Already The Case? Before you look in the Mirror, you Are the Mirror—not a "thing" appeared as separate "knowing-self". It is (in some context and convention of discourse) appropriate to refer to the Inherent Divine Self-Nature, Self-Condition, and Self-State (or fundamental "Root"-Condition) As "Self"—but the Divine Self-Nature, Self-Condition, and Self-State is not "a self" (or an "object"-attending "knowing-self"). Rather, the Divine Self-Nature, Self-Condition, and Self-State Is Self-Existing and Self-Radiant Conscious Light, or Intrinsically egoless Consciousness Itself.

I Am That.

I Am That here—in this midst, and now.

3.

There are no egos in Reality Itself—none. It is not that Adidam is a Way in which you overcome egoity by a process of "wearing it down"—as if emptying water from a boat with a bucket, such that you eventually succeed in getting all of the water out of the boat. There is no water in the boat. There is no ego in the body-mind-complex. There is no ego in Reality Itself. The ego does not, in Reality, exist. There is no separate entity—and the preliminary "Perfect Knowledge" listening-practice points to the non-existence of the otherwise presumed-to-be-separate "knowing-self" (or ego-"I").

If you (as My devotee) engage the preliminary "Perfect Knowledge" listening-practice based on profound devotional recognition-response to Me, turning to Me with all the faculties, you will (inevitably) re-discover, in every moment, that you are not egoically "self"-identified with conditions of any kind. In that case, appearances of a conditional (or psycho-physical) nature—or all apparently "objective" phenomena, whether seemingly "internal" or seemingly "external"—continue to happen, in some apparent sense. But, paradoxically, they happen on the basis of the Intrinsically egoless Divine Self-Nature, Self-Condition, and Self-State and the Transcendental Spiritual Current of Reality Itself, Which "contains" no separate "one". All apparent separateness is, in Reality, a unified field of apparent happening—but without any separate entity that is participating in it or threatened by it.

Such is the "radical" characteristic of the Reality-Way I have Revealed and Given. Such is the "radical" characteristic of the disposition of true devotion to Me. True devotion to Me is (necessarily) ego-transcending. True devotion to Me does not relate to Me as an egoic "other". Only the profoundest devotional recognition of Me can establish profoundest devotion to Me.

4.

As "Narcissus", you live in the checkerboard field, where everyone is gaming, seeking, looking for a goal at one end of the checkerboard or the other, or even just "messing around". You are not even working toward getting out to the edge of the field—and, in fact, there is no edge of the field. There is no center on the checkerboard. You simply move around within it. Thus, there is no separate "self"—but there is also no edge. Thus, the Sphere of the Mirror is Centerless and Boundless. The Mirror has no edges—and, therefore, the Mirror has no center.

The "world" of "object"-reflections is what has tradition-
ally been called "samsara"—the "world" of illusion, the
"world" of suffering. To Most Perfectly Realize the Condition
of the Mirror Itself, Which Is the Perfectly Prior (or Always-
Already) Position, is (in traditional language) "Nirvana"—
or Divine Enlightenment, or Divine Self-Realization. The
Perfectly Prior Position is Perfect. The Perfectly Prior
Position is the seventh stage Realization, Which I Perfectly
Self-Manifest and Perfectly Self-Reveal.

In essence, human society is no different from a beehive
or an ant colony. In a beehive, the queen is simply pumping
out eggs. And the other bees are "designed", in the grid-
pattern of that particular species, to have their particular
functions. Each type of bee has its own genetic and chemi-
cal triggers, as a result of which it acquires a certain appearance and functions in a certain manner. Every bee uncon-
sciously fulfills its pre-patterned role—including its participation in the necessary procedures of replication—and
every bee eventually becomes obsolete, post-replication, in
a pre-determined period of however many days or weeks.

Human society functions in exactly the same manner.
There is a necessary biological replication-process, by which
"replacement organisms" are made—and also a process of
replicating states of mind and states of emotion—and then
you (the temporary link) become obsolete and drop dead.
What you always cling to as "you" is eventually shed, without a moment's hesitation—like excrement. From the "point
of view" of the universe, the "you" that is the body-mind-
complex is nothing but "shit". The "body-mind you" is nothing
but a temporary little event. The "body-mind you" is, in both
cosmic (or conditional) Nature and Reality Itself, not treated as
having any ultimate importance—and, in Truth (or in Reality
Itself), the "body-mind you" has no ultimate importance.

Where is the Freedom from this intolerable bondage? If
you look at your actual situation in this "world", and truly

THE TEACHING MANUAL OF PERFECT SUMMARIES

observe and understand what it is, how could you possibly be naively enthusiastic about it? In and of itself, your situation in this "world" is hell. In and of itself, your situation in this "world" is terrible. If there is anything potentially beautiful about your situation in this "world", you must be (apparently) associated with the "world" from a different position—the Truth-Position, the Reality-Position, the Intrinsic Self-Position That Is (Always Already) Free of the implications of the machine of klik-klak-happening. If this "world" is only repetitive activities and replication—perhaps with a little shift, a minor change, accompanying each gesture, and with the inevitable ending in death—how can that be accepted, except that it is imposed on you by force? What is there of delight in that?

What is greater than that? Is there anything greater? Yes, there Is. But a Reality-Revealer is needed, to make it plain—not only to make it plain through words, but to Be it, to Self-Manifest it, to Show the Way, such that the relationship to That One can become a Way of life for That One's devotees.

What is it about this that the "modern Everyman" cannot accept? Throughout all human history, great beings, in their various modes of Realization, have appeared in the midst of humankind and done exactly this. What is there about all of "modern" you, that you cannot accept this, that you insist on subordinating What is Supremely Great to what is "dark" and "sinful"?

As "Narcissus", your law is to presume your own independence, your own immunity, and your own position of being "in control". Such are the signs of your desperate search for safety and survival—because you tacitly understand, at heart, that you are in trouble in this "shit-maze" here. You want to pretend contentedness—but you are not contented. All egos are inherently disturbed.

Whatever is orderly is the checkerboard itself. To be a square in that checkerboard is to be inherently disturbed—

but you are so bound that your energy of disturbance simply acts as a mover in the game, rather than moving you out of the game. To be in the "self"-knot-position is not Bliss, not Happiness, not Truth, not Divine.

Order is not Truth—nor is disorder. Truth is Perfectly Prior to both order and disorder. When Truth is Self-Established, then a creative process of Right Order—or the working-out of chaotic situations—happens, but only in That Free and Divine Disposition.

If you remain in the checkerboard pattern, it inevitably becomes more and more complex—because the checkerboard is an infinite field, without center or bounds. There is always more and more and more and more and more.

I Am the Hole in the universe, Perfectly Prior to all this mummery. I Am here, to Break the spell, to Make Right Life and the Real Reality-Way possible, in an otherwise deluded context of "world"-happening. However, the ego's impulse is to avoid My Divine Imposition, to casually "play around" in this infinite apparent field of the grid of conditional appearances—un-Illumined, not "Bright", "Thumb"-less, without a clue.

Chaos is also very orderly. If you get down to its up-closest state, you will see: Everything is happening on a checkerboard, a digital screen, a grid. In that sense, everything is orderly. If you step back, you are seeing the piecemeal picture, and it is chaotic—even sometimes appearing to have edges and a center. That is the conditional universe. That is moment to moment ego-existence—feeling that the ego-"I" is the center of the universe, merely because it is the center of its own apparition of grid.

The "point of view" of attention—the fixed locus of attention in the space-time grid—is what you identify as "self". You call it "I". Thus, the grid "point of view" is the origin of the "I"-utterance. From that "point of view", if there were not a checkerboard in which to presume a position, you would not live. There would not be any separate "I". And, in Reality, that is exactly how it is. There is no separate "I".

The only-by-Me Revealed and Given "Radical" Reality-Way of Adidam Ruchiradam is the Way of Reality Itself. The "Radical" Reality-Way of Adidam Ruchiradam begins with Reality Itself—and, therefore, the "Radical" Reality-Way of Adidam Ruchiradam has no goal. Reality Itself Is the Realization Constantly Given by Me in the "Radical" Reality-Way of Adidam Ruchiradam. Ultimately, that Realization is Most Perfect, Outshining all-and-All—but such Most Perfect Realization is simply the Most Perfect Demonstration of That Which Is the Reality-Way from the beginning.

Devotion to Me (utterly turned to Me, with all of the principal faculties) and the "Perfect Knowledge" listening-practice—engaged, in conjunction with each other, in every life-context, in accordance with My Instructions (and, necessarily, supported by the by-Me-Given disciplines of right life)—is the Way of Reality Itself. Therefore, the only-by-Me Revealed and Given "Radical" Reality-Way of Adidam Ruchiradam is Reality-Realizing, in every moment, from the beginning. Really ego-transcending devotional Communion with Me, demonstrated moment to moment through the "Perfect Knowledge" listening-practice (and through the forms of life-discipline I have Given), Is the Non-conditional Realization of Reality Itself. Therefore, in every moment, the practice of the only-by-Me Revealed and Given "Radical" Reality-Way of Adidam Ruchiradam has the virtue of being Established in Reality Itself—rather than being trapped in mummery, in egoity, in fear.

You exist as if you were outside your own body. In Reality, you are not outside your own body—and you are not even merely inside your own body. In Reality, you are Perfectly Prior to the body (and Perfectly Prior to the total psycho-physical ego-"I")—which means that there is no "you". "You" (or "I") is nothing but a reference to a chronically presumed "point of view" in time and space, a mere illusion of "location" on the centerless and boundless checkerboard-grid of the "world"-mummery.

Reality Itself has no position on a grid. Reality Itself Is Perfectly Prior—Prior to center, Prior to bounds, Prior to problem, Prior to seeking, Prior to un-Truth. Reality Itself is Self-Evidently Divine. Reality Itself is All the God There Is.

The "Object-God" is false. The "Object-God" is an illusion. Fundamentally, the "Object-God" is merely a concept, politically and culturally used (in the common "world" of egos) to provide a metaphorical situation for the conventional assertion of "authority", and for the conventional "authoritative" (or "official") pronouncing (and enforcing) of social imperatives.

The "Object-God" is not Reality Itself. Therefore, the "Object-God" is not That Which Is Inherently Divine.

The "Object-God" is like the "I"-thought: It is merely the illusory center of a language-game. The "world" is another such center of a language-game. The "I"-thought (or the presumed-to-be-independent ego-"self"), and the "world", and the "God"-idea are the three fundamental categories of Reality-as-reflection. As such, "ego-'I'", "world-out-there", and "God-everywhere" are the essential categories of egoic bondage—the tripartite package of "world"-mummery. Some people throw out the "God"-idea—but that does not make any difference, because "ego" provides the grid, and "world" provides the mummery. And if the "God"-idea is still entertained, it provides the (socially dictated) "rules of the game". All of that is simply a manifestation (or extension) of ego-mind.

Real (Acausal) God Is Reality Itself. Real (Acausal) God does not have a name. Nevertheless, words can be used—and I do use them, Revealing to you that Real (Acausal) God Is the Divine Self-Nature, Self-Condition, and Self-State That Is Reality Itself, the Intrinsic Self-Nature, Self-Condition,

Self-State, and Source-Condition of all appearances. That "Root"-Condition is egoless, Centerless, Unbounded, Non-conditional, without limitation, and without bondage.

If you would have your life not be about bondage, Reality Itself must Transform your life. The only-by-Me Revealed and Given "Radical" Reality-Way of Adidam Ruchiradam is that "Radical" (or Always "At-the-Root") Transformation of life, Based on Perfectly Prior Establishment In and As Reality Itself.

"Radical" (or always already "at-the-root") devotion to Me and Intrinsically (or tacitly and egolessly) Self-Exercised "Perfect Knowledge"—the twofold fundamental practice within which all the other by-Me-Given practices and disciplines are to be engaged—is the Avatarically by-Me-Given Divine Means whereby life is Transformed (or Made right) by Reality Itself.

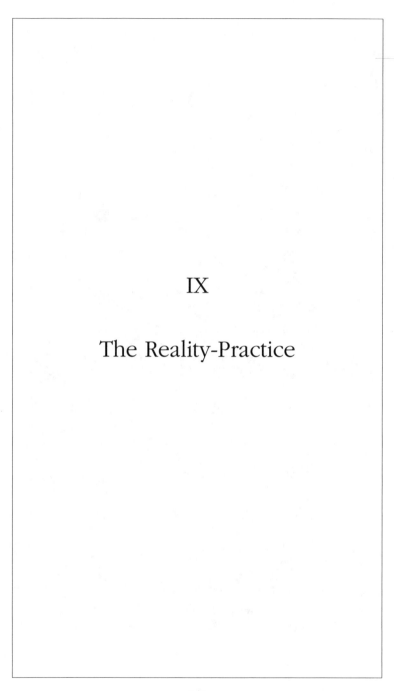

IX

The Reality-Practice

1.

E xcept for Reality Itself, everything is a process of self-replication, or universal reproduction and beginning-less and endless repetition.

Reality Itself <u>Is</u> the Acausal Mirror (or Perfect Reflector) of all-and-All.

All apparent "objects" are merely Reflected (and not otherwise "caused") in the Acausal Mirror That <u>Is</u> Reality Itself.

All apparent "objects" are mere reflections—like a watery mirage.

Apparent "objects"—including every "thing", "world", separate body-mind-"self", living entity, mode of attention, and "point of view"—are not Reality Itself, and are neither necessary nor binding, and are merely apparent, conditionally arising, temporary, non-Ultimate, and not "It".

The body-mind-"self" is like a photographic camera—a "point-of-view"-machine, present to replicate the "object" in view.

The body-mind-"self" constantly makes facsimiles, of "objects" that are either perceived or imagined.

Behind the body-mind-complex is a Perfect Reflector, an Acausal Mirror, Always Already Perfectly Prior to ego-"I", attention, "point of view", "object", reflection, replication, and facsimile.

The body-mind-complex itself is a facsimile-machine—constantly replicating, reproducing, and repeating apparently perceived and otherwise imagined "objects".

The principal "object" that is constantly replicated, reproduced, and repeated in, as, and by means of the body-mind-complex is the "self"-imagined ego-idea, or the illusion of a separate "self".

The (apparently "objectified") "world" is reflection, replication, reproduction, and repetition.

The Intrinsic Self-Nature, Self-Condition, and Self-State of the "world" Is Reality Itself—or Indivisible Conscious Light.

The One and Only Indivisible Conscious Light Is Self-Existing, Self-Radiant, Perfectly Prior, Intrinsically egoless, Non-separate, Non-conditional, Perfectly Non-"objective", and of an Irreducibly Acausal Nature.

All reflected "objects" arise, self-replicate, reproduce, and repeat.

The Self-Reality of Acausal Conscious Light Merely and Always Already Is As Such.

2.

It is only in the imagination that "ego-in-the-world" exists. The separate "self" is simply a "thing" presumed and entertained in mind. Ego is an imagined "objectified" persona. The "self"-image (and the entire drama) of ego is something conceived and believed in mind only, including the minds of apparent "others" who are likewise imagining.

Therefore, the life of the separate "self" is literally an illusion—but the ego-based human being constantly lives in that illusion, constantly re-imagines that illusion, and constantly furthers that illusion in imagination, supported by desire-energy. The mutual association between human beings is association between imagining minds—re-imagining one another, and being imagined by one another—each so-called "individual" perpetually re-imagining itself through mental reflections.

The Reality of existence is something else entirely. The actual situation, the True Self-Nature, Self-Condition, and Self-State, is Perfectly Prior, Non-separate, Indivisible, Self-Existing, and Self-Radiant. That Is the Real Condition. That Real Condition is Self-Evident—and That Real Condition can be Intrinsically and intuitively Self-"Located". The Realization of That Real Condition is a Transcendental Spiritual matter—

but the Nature of Reality, the Real Nature of existence, can, in any moment, be intuitively noticed by anyone.

The only-by-Me Revealed and Given "Radical" Reality-Way of Adidam Ruchiradam is the Real living process of transcending imagination—transcending the imagining of separate-"self"-existence and the mutual re-imagining of separate-"self"-existence. Every apparent individual Really Exists As the Perfectly Prior Self-Nature, Self-Condition, and Self-State, or the Reality-Condition. The imagined separate "knowing-self" is a merely apparent "known-object" (and the otherwise mere "shadow" of a conditional appearance), superimposed on the Perfectly Prior and Inherent Reality-Condition. The imagined ego-life is, thus, "played" on the Perfectly Prior Self-Base of Intrinsically egoless Conscious Light, like a reflection in a mirror.

The practice of the only-by-Me Revealed and Given "Radical" Reality-Way of Adidam Ruchiradam is about transcending the imagined separate "self", or the "self"-imagining and "other"-imagining and "world"-imagining activity of egoity. Fundamentally, the "Radical" Reality-Way of Adidam Ruchiradam is a process of being Attracted (by Me) Beyond such imagining, Beyond the ideas of "self" and "other" and "world" that are imagined (or proposed) in mind only.

Attraction beyond the ego-process (of "self"-imagining and "other"-imagining and "world"-imagining) is whole bodily devotional turning to Me (on the basis of the devotional recognition-response to Me). When devotional recognition-response to Me becomes profound, and (on that basis) whole bodily turning to Me (beyond "self"-contraction, and beyond the contents of the psycho-physically happening imagination) becomes profound, then there is searchless Beholding of Me. Searchless Beholding of Me is true surrender to Me. Searchless Beholding of Me happens by means of the (whole bodily) ego-forgetting turning to Me, not by means of "working on" the ego-"self". In that real (whole bodily) turning to Me, the presumed separate-"self"-activity is transcended.

Thus, devotional turning to Me is not a merely superficial gesture. Rather, devotional turning to Me is a profundity that is moved beyond imagination—beyond the construct of separateness that is constantly being manufactured, as if in a mirror. By means of devotional turning to Me, I am (in due course) "Located" Transcendentally Spiritually. In the searchless Beholding of Me, I am "Known" Transcendentally Spiritually. Even the entire body is Invaded by Me Transcendentally Spiritually—and the "Perfect Knowledge" I have Described is Realized Intrinsically, by Transcendental Spiritual Means alone, as the Transcendental Spiritual State of Reality Itself. Such is the nature of right and true practice of the only-by-Me Revealed and Given "Radical" Reality-Way of Adidam Ruchiradam.

The daily course of ego-bound human beings is a drama lived through the efforts of imagination in mind (or lived as a psycho-physical construct rooted in mind). Thus, the drama of separate "selves" is played out on the basis of mind. However, when Realization of Me is most profound, there is <u>Always</u> <u>Already</u> no mind, no attention, no body, no egoic "self"-identification with any psycho-physical constructs, no ego, no separate "self", no "knowing-subject". There Is Only Self-Evident Reality Itself, Which Is Transcendental and Inherently Spiritual in Nature. Reality Itself has no conditional content whatsoever. Reality Itself Is the "Bright"— or the Self-Existing and Self-Radiant Current of Conscious Light—Which Is Self-Evidently Divine. Reality Itself Is simply the Condition That Is Always Already The Case.

The ego-construct, or the imagined "self", is <u>not</u> Always Already The Case. The ego-construct is like something noticed in a mirror. The ego-construct is an apparent "objectification" of separate "knowing-self", on the "surface" (so to speak) of the Mirror of Conscious Light.

3.

Those who truly practice the only-by-Me Revealed and Given "Radical" Reality-Way of Adidam Ruchiradam are constantly transcending the imagined drama of daily life and egoity. That process allows the profound release of egoic bondage. Therefore, those who truly practice the "Radical" Reality-Way of Adidam Ruchiradam freely and inevitably (on the basis of the always Perfectly Prior transcending of egoity itself) show the evidence of life-transformation—bodily, emotional, and mental transformations, changes, and re-formations—or a process of the rightening of the whole body. This rightening occurs Acausally—on the Basis of That Which Is Perfectly Prior and Indivisible. That Which is Transcendentally Spiritually Transmitted As My Very and Self-Evidently Divine State is Indivisible and all-and-All-Liberating. Thus I (Acausally, or by Means of My Mere Presence) Vanish the ego-patterning of My devotee.

A devotee of Mine who is exemplary in his or her practice is exemplary by virtue of demonstrations of physical, emotional, and mental life-rightening, and by virtue of demonstrations of the Transcendental Spiritual evidence of My Transcendental Spiritual Invasion of his or her bodily person and life. Therefore, the psycho-physical evidence and the Transcendental Spiritual evidence (a dimension of which shows itself through signs of Transcendental Spiritual Invasion of the psycho-physical structure) are the two fundamental characteristics that indicate whether a devotee of Mine is right with Me and exemplary in practice.

My devotees must fit themselves to right devotion to Me, and go through the living ordeal of right practice—moment to moment, and day by day. The process of life-rightening is an ordeal of shedding the ego-pattern, or the imagined persona. Therefore, that process of life-rightening is, necessarily, a process of renunciation. The patterns of egoity are built into the body-mind-complex as psycho-physical tendencies. Therefore, those patterns do not disappear merely because you come up with a notion about changing them. The life-rightening process must be profoundly engaged and persisted in, so that real turning away from, and real shedding of, ego-patterning occurs. That is a fundamental aspect of the "Radical" Reality-Way of Adidam Ruchiradam— the "ordeal" aspect.

The other profound aspect of the only-by-Me Revealed and Given "Radical" Reality-Way of Adidam Ruchiradam is of a Transcendental Spiritual nature—not merely a philosophical process, or a process in mind, but (rather) a process that intrinsically transcends mind (and even all of the body-mind-"self"). The Transcendental Spiritual process of the "Radical" Reality-Way of Adidam Ruchiradam is not what would otherwise be called an "ordeal". The Transcendental Spiritual process of the "Radical" Reality-Way of Adidam Ruchiradam is simply a profundity of Divine Gifts. The Transcendental Spiritual process of the "Radical" Reality-Way of Adidam Ruchiradam is a profound process of the Awakening and the demonstration of "Perfect Knowledge" Itself. Nevertheless, that process must occur in the field of the life of My devotee.

Therefore, My devotees who "Know" Me most profoundly are those who embrace the necessary ordeal of practice most profoundly. Their disposition, moment to moment, is one of turning to Me and Communing with Me, rather than merely being distracted by, and preoccupied with, the imaginary ego-life, the drama of ego-life, the idea of the separate "self" being played out like a cartoon in the psycho-physical mirroring of Reality Itself.

My devotee is turned to Reality Itself—not merely to the constantly imagined drama of separate "self", enacted in the forms of body-mind. The turning from psycho-physical ego-patterning to Me—by Means of Communion with My Very and Self-Evidently Divine State—is what makes the practice of the only-by-Me Revealed and Given "Radical" Reality-Way of Adidam Ruchiradam a true ego-transcending practice (or ordeal). That is the renunciate aspect of the "Radical" Reality-Way of Adidam Ruchiradam. That is what allows the "Locating" and "Knowing" of My Transcendental Spiritual Invasion to Purify, Transform, and Perfectly Awaken My devotee.

Therefore, My devotees are Called (by Me) to a profound life of practice, in which there is profound "self"-understanding relative to the habits and patterns of ego-life that are otherwise imposed on Consciousness Itself. My most profoundly practicing (or mature) devotees are rooted in the Transcendental Spiritual Current of Reality Itself, Which is Avatarically Self-Transmitted by Me and As Me. My such devotees continue to function (in the apparent sense) in the mirrored "world", but without being bound to it through uninspected imagination. The merely patterned life is not the basis for the day to day or moment to moment existence of My rightly practicing devotees. Rather, Reality Itself is the Context of the apparent life for My truly and rightly practicing devotees—and, most especially, for those who are entered into true Transcendental Spiritual Communion with Me as a moment to moment life-practice.

4.

I Appear here in psycho-physical Form—but My Self-Confession and Self-Revelation to you is that there is no separate "self" associated with This apparent Body of Mine. This Body of Mine is not thinking, is not present in the form of attention, is not associated with a separate consciousness. My Own "Bright" Divine State—Thus Exemplified, even in apparent Coincidence with physical existence—is a Demonstration and a Revelation to My devotees (and to all beings) about the Nature of Reality Itself, and how Reality Itself Appears when It is Coincident with what is otherwise ordinary psycho-physical human existence.

My Bodily Incarnation here is to Provide the Avataric Agent for Divine Self-"Emergence" and Divine Self-Revelation—and, on That Basis, to Provide the ongoing focus for My devotees, such that My Transcendental Spiritual Self-Transmission can be Perpetuated in this "world". Therefore, This Body, photographed (and otherwise recorded) during My Divine Avataric physical human Lifetime, Provides the "Image" (or Me-"Representation") for the focus of the faculties in My devotees—both while I am physically Alive and after My Divine Avataric physical human Lifetime. My Avatarically-Born bodily (human) Divine Form is a Forever Revelation—but It is not an "object". If you devotionally recognize Me, you "Know" Me As I Am—not as an "object", not through appearances, not as an "other", or (even) the "Other". Therefore, you transcend all of the imagining of the "separate-self-object"—the "I-object" that is the basis of the moment to moment life of ego-imagining—by whole bodily turning to Me and devotionally recognizing Me As I Am.

Devotees approach Me through Invocation of Me by Name and through regard of My Avatarically-Born bodily (human) Divine Form (whether directly or in My "Representation"-Form). If they do not approach Me rightly, they are approaching Me as an "objective other". In that case, I am a "known-object" to them—just as the persona of separate "knowing-self" is, for them, a "known-object", or an "objectification" associated with attention. If attention were not associated with the presumed psycho-physical construct, the "objectified self", the mirrored "self"-idea, there would only be the Self-Evident Reality of Indivisible Conscious Light Itself.

Therefore, in their turning to Me, My devotees are turned away from all the patterning of the faculties, which govern life through egoic identification with an imagined persona of separate "self". However, in their turning to Me,

My devotees are not merely turning to an "object", or to an "objective other". Rather, My devotees' turning to Me is the means whereby the contents of the reflected (or "knowing") "self" are forgotten. In that turning to Me, there is the intrinsic entering into My "Bright" Divine Self-Condition—and that entering into My Condition is profoundly Established by My Transcendental Spiritual Self-Transmission of My "Bright" Divine State.

Therefore, the fullness of the process of the only-by-Me Revealed and Given "Radical" Reality-Way of Adidam Ruchiradam is beyond the Second Congregation student-beginner base-adaptation to the functional, practical, relational, and cultural disciplines, and to the fundamental practice of devotion to Me, and to the preliminary listening-practice of "Perfect Knowledge". The fully established practice of the "Radical" Reality-Way of Adidam Ruchiradam is a Transcendental Spiritual matter, in intrinsic Communion with Me, and lived in accordance with My Instructions of how to maintain ego-transcending Transcendental Spiritual Communion with Me.

Therefore, the fully established practice of the only-by-Me Revealed and Given "Radical" Reality-Way of Adidam Ruchiradam is not merely about receiving something Spiritually in the midst of your ego-based imagined life. Rather, the fully established practice of the only-by-Me Revealed and Given "Radical" Reality-Way of Adidam Ruchiradam is a matter of uninterruptedly turning away from the imagined ego-"object" and steadily onwardly turning to Me. In that turning to Me, My devotee not only forgets the ego-"object" (or the "objectified self" and its drama), but enters egolessly into My "Bright" Divine State.

If I am related to merely as an "objective other", there is no entering into My "Bright" Divine State. In that case, there is simply the turning toward some "objective" appearance. Therefore, My devotee must not turn to Me merely as an "objective" form. My "Image" (or Me-"Representation") is not merely a "thing" in your Communion Hall. I am not merely an imagined or remembered appearance. All the apparently "objective" sacred Means I have Given—including Simple Name-Invocation of Me, and the Beholding of My "Representation"-Form—are simply Means for turning from the imagined (or "objectified") ego-"I" and its drama, and turning to Me, and (thereby) entering into My "Bright" Divine State, the Field of My Transcendentally Spiritually Self-Transmitted Perfectly Prior Self-Condition. In the process of truly profoundly engaging of this by-Me-Given practice, the ego-pattern is released—and replaced by true renunciation. On the basis of this profundity of practice and renunciation (altogether), there is the Realization of Transcendentally Spiritually Awakened Conscious Existence in the Inherent (or Perfectly Prior and Acausal) Form of Reality Itself.

5.

The social interactions between people are, fundamentally, ego-based—ego-bound and ego-binding. Those interactions are about the mutual exercise of habits of imagination—the imagining of the "objectified" ego-life, the life of separate entities (or separate beings). However, the life of separateness is simply not true—because it is not (in and of itself) Real. In Reality Itself, the life of separateness is merely a reflected and "self"-imagined "object". All the while, and Always Already, There Is the Self-Existing and Self-Radiant Indivisible Conscious Light. Conscious Light Is All—and all-and-All. My true devotees are established in That—and, then, the reflected "world", or the apparently "objectified" (or conditionally apparent) "world", has an entirely different characteristic than that which is presumed on the ego-basis.

When the "world" is seen in Reality, life is a very different matter than it is when the "world" is seen from "point of view"—or "objectified", as in a mirror.

My true devotees are entered into (and, in due course, Perfectly Identified with) the Self-Position of the Mirror—rather than being engaged merely in "playing" among the reflections, as if the reflections (rather than the Mirror Itself) were Reality Itself. This entering (and, in due course, Perfect Identification) is not merely a philosophical exercise—but it is a matter of right, true, and consistent Reality-Practice.

The only-by-Me Revealed and Given "Radical" Reality-Way of Adidam Ruchiradam is the Reality-Way of Transcendental Spirituality—or, in other words, the Reality-Way of Intrinsically ego-Transcending Spirituality. The "Radical" Reality-Way of Adidam Ruchiradam is not merely a technique engaged by egos—or psycho-physically "objectified" presumed "points of view" that move about and interact. The Transcendental Spirituality of the only-by-Me Revealed and Given "Radical" Reality-Way of Adidam Ruchiradam is Self-"Located" (by Means of My Divine Avataric Transcendental Spiritual Grace) as a Profundity of the Intrinsic Prior State, based upon the devotional practice of turning beyond the ego-"self" (and the apparently "objectified", or mirrored, contents of the presumed-to-be separate entity).

The profundity of devotion to Me—associated with, and expressed in, the range of functional, practical, relational, and cultural disciplines that are required from the very beginning of practice in the "Radical" Reality-Way of Adidam Ruchiradam—is essential to the preliminary listening-practice of "Perfect Knowledge". When all of that is matured to the point of constancy and essential psycho-physical equanimity, coincident with the preliminary listening-practice of "Perfect Knowledge", then there is the entering into the profundity of the only-by-Me Revealed and Given "Radical" Reality-Way of Adidam Ruchiradam, which is searchless Beholding of Me and ego-transcending Transcendental Spiritual Communion with Me. In that case, the preliminary listening-practice of "Perfect Knowledge" becomes a

Transcendental Spiritual Revelation. Then "Perfect Knowledge" is Transcendentally Spiritually Transmitted (by Means of My Divine Avataric Transcendental Spiritual Grace) as the State of Reality Itself.

The fundamental exercise of the "Radical" Reality-Way of Adidam Ruchiradam (Which Is the Reality-Way of "Perfect Knowledge") is whole bodily (and truly ego-forgetting) turning to Me. On that basis, the moment to moment preliminary listening-practice of "Perfect Knowledge" becomes appropriate, but only in the context of the devotional turning to Me, which (in due course) becomes searchless Beholding of Me. Therefore, "Perfect Knowledge" Itself is Demonstrated by My Transcendental Spiritual Self-Transmission of My "Bright" Divine State to My ego-forgetting devotee. Then I am tangibly "Located". I Invade, or "Crash Down" upon, the bodily apparent entity of My devotee, and That In-Filling Manifests As the Self-Evidence of Reality Itself.

The "Perfect Knowledge" of Reality Itself is not merely a philosophical matter. The "Perfect Knowledge" of Reality Itself is not merely about inversion upon the Consciousness Principle (in the sixth stage manner). Rather, the "Perfect Knowledge" of Reality Itself is about Establishment of the Perfectly Prior Self-Nature, Self-Condition, and Self-State of Reality Itself, by Means of the Transcendental Spiritual Self-Transmission of Reality Itself.

When My devotees fully and rightly approach Me, on the basis of the searchless Beholding of Me, and actually "Locate" Me and "Know" Me Transcendentally Spiritually via (and also Perfectly Prior to) the whole body, then they will understand that What I am Saying Is Truth. They will have the exact and Inherently Irrefutable Evidence, because they will comprehend the precise distinction between merely philosophical (and, necessarily, ego-based) notions of "Perfect Knowledge" and the Transcendental Spiritual Self-Evidence of "Perfect Knowledge". The Transcendental

Self-Evidence of "Perfect Knowledge" is the Inherently Irrefutable Transcendental Spiritual Self-Evidence of Reality Itself—and not merely a "subjectively" idealized mode of the interior of apparent psycho-physical awareness.

My Transcendental Spiritual Self-Transmission Proves, Gives, and Demonstrates "Perfect Knowledge" as a Transcendental Spiritual Fact—Perfectly Prior to all conditionality, and Perfectly Prior to egoity. Therefore, in due course, My Transcendental Spiritual Transmission of the Divine Self-Nature, Self-Condition, and Self-State Awakens the "Perfect Practice" of the Reality-Way of "Perfect Knowledge". The "Perfect Practice" is Awakened by Transcendental Spiritual Means alone—but that Awakening to the "Perfect Practice" of the Reality-Way of "Perfect Knowledge" is also associated with the life-rightening process of functional, practical, relational, and cultural disciplines, coincident with the fullness of whole bodily devotional turning to Me, and (also) with the "conscious process" of the preliminary listening-practice of "Perfect Knowledge", and (indeed) with all the Means I have Given as an art of ego-renouncing life-practice. Nevertheless, the Event and Process of Realization is entirely of a Transcendental Spiritual Nature—Perfectly Prior to all conditionality, and all ego-effort, and all imagined separateness.

"Perfect Knowledge" Itself, and the "Perfect Practice" of It, coincides with perfect renunciation (or the perfect transcending of egoity). That is the responsibility of My devotee. If My devotee is thus responsible, then My devotee is available to the Most Perfect Realization of My Transcendentally Spiritually Transmitted (and Self-"Bright") Divine State.

X

Transcendental
(and Non-Conditional)
Spirituality

1.

To focus one-pointedly on a mantra (or any prescribed sacred utterance), or on a sacred Name, or on the "I"-thought, or on any thought whatsoever—to the exclusion of all other thoughts—is a strategic form of mental concentration. When the strategic concentration of mind is methodically applied in order to focus attention (and thought) on its own Transcendental source, the effort is a sixth stage exercise—an exclusionary "method" of Transcendental concentration, founded upon the presumption (and even the presumed "problem") of the ego-"I" (or the "knowing-self"). Characteristically, all sixth stage "methods" are exercises of strategic (or goal-oriented) concentration of mental attention. As such, sixth stage "methods" (like the otherwise strategic "methods" associated with each and all of the first six, or ego-based, stages of life) involve, as a procedural first step, the effort, or strategy, of mind-control. Thus, the general sixth stage rule of procedure is as follows: First, you concentrate on one particular thought—thus and thereby excluding all other thoughts—and, then (or on that basis), you "locate" the source of that one particular and exclusive thought. That procedure, process, technique, or general sixth stage "method" is not the practice of Intrinsic (or Tacit and Unmediated) Self-Apprehension (or of Intrinsically Self-Apperceived Self-Identification), but (rather) that exclusive sixth stage "method" involves a step in-between that is dissociatively introversive (or strategically non-participatory), and that is mediated (or made both conditional and indirect) by means of the introduction of the presumption of an "inwardly-objectified subjectivity" (or the "knowing-self", and the mind of "knowing", and of "knowledge", and of the "known"), and the subsequent introduction of some kind of an "objectified" idea (or mind-form, or conceptual "object") as the necessary instrument of the "method".

The preliminary "Perfect Knowledge" listening-practice of the only-by-Me Revealed and Given "Radical" Reality-Way of Adidam Ruchiradam has a "root"-characteristic that is different from the sixth stage protocol. Whereas the sixth stage protocol is, essentially, a strategic (or goal-oriented) and exclusionary technique of Transcendental concentration, the preliminary "Perfect Knowledge" listening-practice is the Direct (or Unmediated) Event of Intrinsic Transcendental (and Intrinsically egoless) Self-Identification (or Self-Intuition, or Self-Apprehension, or Self-Apperception).

The preliminary "Perfect Knowledge" listening-practice simply, tacitly, or without mental exclusiveness or mediation, proceeds as follows: <u>Whatever</u> "known-object" arises, or <u>whatever</u> form of conditional "knowledge" arises, or <u>whatever</u> form of "knowing-subject" may seem to be implied, That Which is <u>not</u> a "known-object", and <u>not</u> any form of a "knowing-self", but Which <u>Is</u> Only (and Perfectly Priorly) the "Perfect Knower" Itself, is to be Intrinsically Self-Identified (or tacitly Self-"Located"). Thus, in the preliminary "Perfect Knowledge" listening-practice, there is no particular "known-object", and no form of conditional "knowledge" (such as the "I"-thought), and no mode or idea or feeling of a "knowing-self" which you are to concentrate upon (or use as a means to exclude all other thoughts). In the right exercise of the preliminary "Perfect Knowledge" listening-practice, there is, simply and tacitly, the Inherently Unmediated Event of Transcendental Self-Identification (or of Intrinsic Self-Intuition), moment to moment—<u>whatever</u> may otherwise arise, in any moment, as "known-object", or form of conditional "knowledge", or mode of an apparent "knowing-self".

Therefore, in the characteristic sixth stage protocol, a mental "object" (such as the "I"-thought) is strategically introduced, in order to concentrate attention exclusively—and, then, the Transcendental source of that exclusive thought is sought, by means of the inversion of attention. In contrast, in the preliminary "Perfect Knowledge" listening-practice of the only-by-Me Revealed and Given "Radical" Reality-Way of Adidam Ruchiradam, no mental "object", or even any "known-object" at all, is introduced as a mediating means to "Locate" the Intrinsically Self-Evident Transcendental Self-Nature, Self-Condition, and Self-State. Rather, whatever (and no matter what) mental or other "known-object" (or conditionally apparent form of "knowledge") may otherwise arise to attention in any particular moment, the Intrinsically Self-Evident Transcendental Self-Nature, Self-Condition, and Self-State is, simply, tacitly Self-"Located"— without the introduction of any mediating means, or any conditionally exercised effort of concentration-"method", or any search to invert attention. Indeed, in the preliminary "Perfect Knowledge" listening-practice of the only-by-Me Revealed and Given "Radical" Reality-Way of Adidam Ruchiradam, the "exercise" is always Perfectly Prior to attention, rather than in and by means of the effort, concentration, or exercise of attention itself.

This is to be understood as a fundamental characteristic of the preliminary "Perfect Knowledge" listening-practice of the only-by-Me Revealed and Given "Radical" Reality-Way of Adidam Ruchiradam—and this characteristic accounts for why the preliminary "Perfect Knowledge" listening-practice is entirely compatible with moment to moment participatory existence, in all circumstances, and under all conditions. Thus, the preliminary "Perfect Knowledge" listening-practice does not require any kind of strategic seclusion—or, indeed, any dissociative orientation or exclusive concentration whatsoever. The preliminary "Perfect Knowledge" listening-practice is not about seeking—nor is it about any form of avoidance. When it is rightly engaged, the preliminary "Perfect Knowledge" listening-practice is entirely coincident with the naturalness of ordinary moment to moment existence—and, therefore, the preliminary "Perfect Knowledge" listening-practice is to be engaged not only (or exclusively) in the necessary periods of daily formal meditation, but it is (also necessarily) to be engaged, moment to moment, outside the occasions (and the sacred and sacramental settings) of formal meditation. Whatever arises conditionally as "known-object", or form of "knowledge", or mode of a "knowing-self", tacitly Self-"Locate" That Which is not an "object"—tacitly Self-"Locate" (or Intrinsically Self-Intuit) That Which is the Non-conditional, Non-"objective", Inherently Non-separate, and Intrinsically egoless Transcendental Spiritual "Perfect Knower".

In the preliminary "Perfect Knowledge" listening-practice, there is no intervening thought on which to concentrate. Therefore, the preliminary "Perfect Knowledge" listening-practice can be engaged in any and every moment, because that practice does not "interfere" (so to speak) with the naturalness (or even the otherwise exercised concentration efforts) of moment to moment participatory existence.

When the preliminary "Perfect Knowledge" listening-practice is entered into most profoundly, the "Perfect Knowledge" That is thus and thereby Self-"Located" has (Itself) nothing to do with "known-objects" and forms of conditional "knowledge". In every moment of its tacit establishment (or of the Intrinsic Self-"Locating" of That Which is not an "object"), the preliminary "Perfect Knowledge" listening-practice intrinsically (rather than strategically and conditionally) transcends all "known-objects", all forms of conditional "knowledge", and all modes of a "knowing-self". That practice is such that it is always already transcending "known-objects"—rather than strategically avoiding "known-objects", or dissociating from them, and (likewise) rather than seeking "known-objects", or any forms of conditional "knowledge", or any modes of a "knowing-self". The preliminary "Perfect Knowledge" listening-practice is not at all associated with the disposition of avoiding-and-seeking. The preliminary

"Perfect Knowledge" listening-practice is simply the Self-Magnification of the Inherent Disposition, That is Always Already Perfectly Prior to "known-objects", Always Already Perfectly Prior to forms of conditional "knowledge", and Always Already Perfectly Prior to the conditional "knower". Therefore, the preliminary "Perfect Knowledge" listening-practice is truly a moment to moment practice, because that practice is perfectly compatible with—and not, in any sense, alien to—moment to moment participatory living.

Indeed, none of the practices of the only-by-Me Revealed and Given "Radical" Reality-Way of Adidam Ruchiradam are dissociative or exclusionary or non-participatory. The preliminary "Perfect Knowledge" listening-practice does not, itself, involve any of the orientation of "how to succeed at conditional existence". Nevertheless, the preliminary "Perfect Knowledge" listening-practice is not incompatible with the naturalness of conditional participatory existence. And all other modes of the practice of the "Radical" Reality-Way of Adidam Ruchiradam are compatible (and always to be made coincident) with the preliminary "Perfect Knowledge" listening-practice. The preliminary "Perfect Knowledge" listening-practice is based upon devotional recognition-response to Me—which is, itself, non-exclusionary, or non-dissociative, in its disposition. By its very nature, devotional recognition-response to Me simply feels beyond—and thus transcends—the binding patterns otherwise associated with the psycho-physical faculties.

Altogether, the various dimensions of the total practice of the "Radical" Reality-Way of Adidam Ruchiradam (which, ultimately, leads to the "Perfect Practice" of "Perfect Knowledge") all take place in the non-dissociative and non-exclusionary (or inherently participatory) context of moment to moment existence.

My Essential Instruction relative to the preliminary "Perfect Knowledge" listening-practice is descriptively Stated, by Me, in a form that tacitly presumes there is the arising of "known-objects", or modes of conditional "knowledge". Thus, I Say, "No matter what 'known-object' or mode of conditional 'knowledge' arises, Intrinsically (tacitly, without resort to any mediating act of thought and attention) Self-'Locate' the Transcendentally Self-Existing and Spiritually Self-Radiant 'Perfect Knower' (or That Which is not a 'known-object' and not a 'knowing-subject')." As such, My very Description of the preliminary "Perfect Knowledge" listening-practice presumes that there is the moment to moment noticing of "known-objects", and modes of conditional "knowledge", and modes of the presumption of a "knowing-self"—as they arise.

The preliminary "Perfect Knowledge" listening-practice is not a matter of strategically diverting attention (by means of a mediating mind-form), in order to dis-"Locate" (or dissociate) attention from all other "objects", as a preliminary strategic means for, thereafter, directing attention toward the Transcendental Spiritual Self-Nature, Self-Condition, and Self-State. Rather, I have Revealed that the Transcendental Spiritual Self-Nature, Self-Condition, and Self-State is Always Already (or tacitly, and Inherently, or Intrinsically, or Priorly—and, thus, Perfectly Prior to any strategic act of attention) Self-"Locatable" under any and all conditions, no matter what arises (or does not arise) as "known-object", or mode of conditional "knowledge", or mode of a "knowing-self".

The Transcendental Spiritual Self-Nature, Self-Condition, and Self-State can always be tacitly (or Non-mentally, and Intrinsically) Self-"Located". It makes absolutely no difference what arises. It makes no difference what kind of "known-object" arises or does not arise, or what mode of conditional "knowledge" arises or does not arise, or what mode or kind of a "knowing-self" arises or does not arise. Therefore, no mediating or strategically exclusive mental or other "object" need be (or even should be) introduced into the Transcendental Spiritual practice—because, in any case, the tacitly

Self-Evident Transcendental Spiritual Self-Nature, Self-Condition, and Self-State is always Intrinsically Self-"Locatable".

2.

I have not only Revealed and Given the Teaching of the Reality-Way of the right practice of Intrinsic Self-"Location" (or Intrinsic Self-Intuition), but I Intrinsically and Purposively Transmit, to My true devotees, the Transcendental Spiritual Current of Self-Apprehension That Is the Avatarically by-Me-Revealed and by-Me-Given Divine Self-Revelation (and Divine Self-Revealer) of the Intrinsically Self-Existing Self-Nature, Self-Condition, and Self-State of Conscious Light (or the "Bright"). Therefore, in due course, the combined exercise of the devotionally responsive turning of the bodily, emotional, mental, and breathing faculties to Me and the preliminary "Perfect Knowledge" listening-practice—necessarily, coincident with all the by-Me-Given (and necessary) disciplines of right life—becomes a Transcendental Spiritual process, in-Filled by Me.

The "Radical" Reality-Way of Adidam Ruchiradam is not merely a philosophical exercise—nor is the "Radical" Reality-Way of Adidam Ruchiradam any kind of effort to exclude everything presumed to be "other than" Consciousness.

Reality Itself does not exclude.

Reality Itself Is As Is.

The Realization of Reality Itself is simply the tacit Self-Realization of That Which Is Always Already The Case—Perfectly Subjectively. There is no ultimate "difference" between that which is apparently "subjective" (or "inside") and that which is apparently "objective" (or "outside"). Most Ultimately, it is Realized that There Is Only and Indivisibly That Which Is Perfectly Subjective—or the Intrinsically Self-Evident Non-conditional Nature, Condition, and State of Conscious Light (Which Is Self-Evidently, or Inherently, Divine).

Reality Itself is not a "Deity".

Truth Itself is not a "God".

Reality Itself (or Truth Itself) Is As Is.

Reality Itself (or Truth Itself) Is Inherently Divine—but Reality Itself (or Truth Itself) is not a "Deity", nor what could (conventionally) be called a "God".

Real (Acausal) God is not an "Other" or an "Object".

Real (Acausal) God Is Reality Itself.

Real (Acausal) God (or Reality Itself, or Truth Itself) is to be Always, and Always Already, and Always Intrinsically Self-"Located" and Self-Realized.

Real (Acausal) God (or Reality Itself, or Truth Itself) is to be Always, and Always Already, and Always Intrinsically Self-"Located" and Self-Realized by the Divine Acausal Means of the only-by-Me and only-As-Me Avatarically Self-Transmitted Divine Transcendental Spiritual Current of Self-Apprehension.

The "Bright"—the Indivisible Divine Self-Nature, Self-Condition, and Self-State of One, and Only, and Non-conditional, and Non-separate, and Intrinsically egoless Conscious Light—is to be Always, and Always Already, and Always Intrinsically Self-"Located" and Self-Realized As Is, whatever arises or does not arise.

The only-by-Me and only-As-Me Avatarically Self-Transmitted Divine Gift of the "Thumbs" Is the Perfect Means That Perfectly Enables the Most Perfect (or seventh stage) Fulfillment of the Transcendental Spiritual Reality-Way of the "Bright" (Which Is the only-by-Me Revealed and Given "Radical" Reality-Way of Adidam Ruchiradam).

3.

The fourth-to-fifth stage traditions characteristically speak of Reality (and of the Real process of existence) as Spiritual in Nature. The sixth stage traditions largely abandon Spiritual language—speaking, instead, of Reality (and of the Real process of existence) as Transcendental in Nature. In contrast to both the fourth-to-fifth stage traditions and the sixth stage traditions, I have Revealed that Reality (and the Real process of existence) is Inherently both Spiritual and Transcendental—and, altogether, Divine—in Nature. Thus, the only-by-Me Revealed and Given seventh stage Reality-Way (Which is the only-by-Me Revealed and Given "Radical" Reality-Way of Adidam Ruchiradam) is both Spiritual and Transcendental—and, altogether, Divine.

The only-by-Me Revealed and Given "Radical" Reality-Way of Adidam Ruchiradam is not to be identified with the fourth-to-fifth stage development (or supposed fulfillment) of the Spiritual process—nor is the only-by-Me Revealed and Given "Radical" Reality-Way of Adidam Ruchiradam to be identified with the sixth stage development (or supposed fulfillment) of the Transcendental process. The only-by-Me Revealed and Given "Radical" Reality-Way of Adidam Ruchiradam extends through and Beyond both the fourth-to-fifth stage (Spiritual) process and the sixth stage (Transcendental) process. In the only-by-Me Revealed and Given "Radical" Reality-Way of Adidam Ruchiradam, the ultimate dimensions of the Spiritual process are demonstrated in the seventh stage context of the Transcendental process (of the "Perfect Practice" of the only-by-Me Revealed and Given "Radical" Reality-Way of Adidam Ruchiradam). The seventh stage fulfillment of Transcendental Self-Realization as a Spiritual process is not communicated or demonstrated in the traditions of the sixth stage Sages. Indeed, the fulfillment of the Spiritual process in the context of the Transcendental process is one of the principal signs of the Uniqueness of the only-by-Me Revealed and Given (and, altogether, seventh stage) "Radical" Reality-Way of Adidam Ruchiradam.

In the sixth stage traditions, there is, sometimes, an affirmation of the relevance, and even the necessity, of Spiritual Transmission in the context of (fourth-to-fifth stage) preparatory dimensions of practice and process that are <u>preliminary</u> to the specifically Transcendental practice and process.

In contrast to the sixth stage traditions, the essential characteristic of the "Perfect Practice" (Itself)—and of seventh stage Divine Self-Realization (Which <u>Is</u> the Inherently Most Perfect Fulfillment of the "Perfect Practice") in the only-by-Me Revealed and Given "Radical" Reality-Way of Adidam Ruchiradam—is the <u>Coincidence</u> and the <u>Non-"difference"</u> between the Transcendental and the Spiritual, or the Dimension of Consciousness and the Dimension of Energy (or Light).

There Is Only One Reality and Truth—and It is not divisible. That Which is at the "root" of all apparent "subjectivity" is, in Truth, or in Reality Itself, Transcendental (and Intrinsically egoless) in Nature. That Which is (otherwise) apparently "objective" (whether "internally" or "externally" perceived or conceived) is, in Truth, or in Reality Itself, Spiritual (and Indivisible) in Nature (or of the Nature of All-Pervading Energy). In the only-by-My-Divine-Avataric-Transcendental-Spiritual-Grace-Given Establishment of the Realization of the seventh stage of life, the Non-"difference" between Consciousness and Energy—or, in other words, the Non-"difference" between the Transcendental and the Spiritual—is Intrinsically Self-Evident. Indeed, the Non-"difference" between Consciousness and Energy—or the Non-conditional and Indivisible Nature of Reality <u>As</u> Conscious Light—is the Very <u>Context</u> of the only-by-Me Revealed and Given seventh stage Realization.

The Truth That is at the "root" of all apparent "subjectivity" is Transcendental. The Truth That is apparently "objective" is Spiritual. And, in Reality, there is no "difference" between Transcendental and Spiritual—or between the "root" of the apparently "subjective" and the otherwise apparently "objective". Transcendental and Spiritual <u>Are</u>—in Truth, or in Reality Itself—Indivisible, Non-separate, and Non-"different". The Transcendental Self-Condition of every apparent "subjective entity" is utterly Non-egoic and Non-separate—and, similarly, the Spiritual Self-Condition of all apparent "objects" (whether "internal" or "external") is utterly Non-individuated and Non-differentiated.

4.

There Is Only <u>One</u> Absolute Reality and Truth—Which Is Non-"different", Transcendental, Inherently Spiritual, and Self-Evidently Divine. The One Reality and Truth Is the One and Indivisible Conscious Light. Such is the Nature of Most Perfect (or seventh stage) Realization. Therefore, Divine Realization <u>Is</u>—Really and Necessarily—Self-Realization. And Perfect Self-Realization <u>Is</u>—Really and Necessarily—Divine Realization (or the Non-"different" Self-Realization of Acausal Real God).

The Transcendental Nature of Reality is suggestively incorporated into the idealism of the fourth-to-fifth stage traditions—especially in terms of the notion of the Indivisibility of the Divine. Nevertheless, in the fourth-to-fifth stage traditions, there is no right development of the full and specific Transcendental aspect of Realization.

Similarly, the Spiritual process is, sometimes, acknowledged, by the Sages of the sixth stage traditions, to be a necessary preliminary to the Transcendental process. Nevertheless, the sixth stage traditions do not, altogether, fully or sufficiently coincide with the Real Spiritual process of existence. The (exclusionary) sixth stage orientation is fundamentally disposed to divorce itself from the Spiritual process, and (thereby) to make the process of Realization into a "consideration" in the presumed (and exclusive) "subjective" (or "knowing-self") domain of Consciousness, without reference to Energy (or Light) or Spirituality (and the Spiritual process).

The non-Spiritual disposition that is characteristic of the sixth stage traditions does not represent the Real process of Perfect Reality-Realization. In Truth, the sixth stage process (or that stage and dimension of the traditional process of Realization that would transcend all the limitations of "subjective" content) can only be <u>fully</u> accomplished by <u>Transcendental</u> <u>Spiritual</u> Means.

In Truth, or in Reality Itself, the right, true, and full Transcendental process of Reality-Realization is not (and cannot be) merely a philosophical exercise. It is only when the Transcendental process is Perfectly Fulfilled—necessarily, by My Avatarically Self-Transmitted Divine Spiritual Means—that the Transcendental process can become the only-by-Me Revealed and Given seventh stage Realization.

The fulfillment of the Transcendental process by Spiritual Means is a fundamental—and fundamentally Unique—characteristic of the only-by-Me Revealed and Given seventh stage "Radical" Reality-Way of Adidam Ruchiradam. The only-by-Me Revealed and Given seventh stage of life is—Uniquely—a Spiritually-Realized (and Spiritually Self-Evident) Transcendental Realization. The only-by-Me Revealed and Given seventh stage Realization is—Uniquely—Indivisible and Non-"different". The only-by-Me Revealed and Given seventh stage of life is—Uniquely—the Most Perfect (or Transcendental, Inherently Spiritual, Intrinsically egoless, and Self-Evidently Divine) Realization of Reality Itself.

The fourth-to-fifth stage Yogis and Saints characteristically speak of the Spiritual Nature of Reality—and, especially, of the Spiritual Nature of all "objects" (both "internal" and "external").

The sixth stage Sages characteristically speak of the Transcendental Nature of Reality—and, especially, of the Transcendental Nature of the "non-objective root" of the "subjective" (or "knowing-self") condition.

I (Alone) Declare and Reveal the Spiritual-and-Transcendental Nature of Reality—even in the context of whatever is conditionally apparent (whether "internally", or "externally", or in any sense "objectively", or in any manner "subjectively").

I (Alone) Declare and Reveal the Spiritual-and-Transcendental Nature of the seventh stage process of Most Perfect Realization of the One and Indivisible Conscious Light (or the "Bright") That Is Reality Itself.

I (Alone) Avatarically Self-Reveal and Avatarically Self-Transmit the Divine Transcendental Spiritual Self-Nature, Self-Condition, and Self-State—As and by Means of the Self-Existing and Self-Radiant Divine Transcendental Spiritual Current (or the "Thumbs") of the Transcendental Divine Self-Apprehension of the Self-Existing and Self-Radiant Self-Nature, Self-Condition, and Self-State of Conscious Light (or the "Bright").

XI

The Root-Characteristics
of Intrinsic Self-Understanding
of Reality Itself

I.

1. All "objects" are not-"self".

2. All "objects" are the conventionally-presumed and psychologically-inferred relations of a "self"-concretized space-time-"location"—or a "point of view", exercising itself as observing-attention, and, thus and thereby, selectively "objectifying" whatever apparently arises, by coincidently and reflexively referring all "objects" to a categorically presumed, but never actually "experienced", or discretely indicated, "self"-entity (or ego-"I").

3. A space-time-"location", functioning as all-"objectifying" attention, is not a "self", or a categorically existing "subjective" entity (or "self-object").

4. There is no "self-object", or intrinsic, particular, and discretely "differentiated" ego-entity—no space-time-"located", or "point-of-view"-limited, separate, independent, and discretely discernible, or specifically definable, "self"-identity, or "inner subject", or ego-"I".

5. There are no Really-existing "objects"—no separate and independent "outer-objective" or "inner-objective" forms, states, or "things".

6. All apparent "objects" are psychologically inferred to exist with reflexive "subjective" reference to a coincidently inferred "inner self-identity" that is never "experientially" defined and "known", and that does not, itself, Really exist.

7. There Is Only Intrinsically egoless, Intrinsically "object-less", Perfectly Indivisible, Perfectly Non-separate, and Perfectly Acausal Reality Itself.

II.

Consciousness Itself is not the "subject" in relation to any "object".

Consciousness Itself <u>Is</u> Intrinsically and Always Already Perfectly Prior to all "objects".

Consciousness Itself <u>Is</u> Intrinsically Free of egoic "self"-identification with any and all "objects".

All "objects" are <u>not</u> "self"—or <u>not</u> the "object"-apprehending "point of view".

All "objects" are apparent <u>relations</u> of the "point of view" that apprehends them.

All "objects" are the apparent relations of functional attention—which does not, itself, constitute a "self".

Consciousness Itself <u>Is</u> Always Already (or Intrinsically and Perfectly) Prior to "point of view" (or attention itself)—and, Thus, Intrinsically Prior to the psychologically-inferred observing-and-responding separate "self"-identity, or the "subjectively"-inferred pseudo-relation (or fictional "subject") of apparent "objects".

Consciousness Itself <u>Is</u> Transcendentally Self-Existing, egoless, Indivisible, Non-separate, Acausal, Non-"objective", Intrinsically Without "object", Perfectly Subjective, Without "self-location", Perfectly Prior to the characteristic of relatedness, and Spiritually Self-Radiant.

Consciousness Itself <u>Is</u> the Mere and Perfectly relationless Witness of all-and-All.

Consciousness Itself <u>Is</u> the One and Indivisible Conscious Light That <u>Is</u> the Self-Nature, Self-Condition, and Self-State That <u>Is</u> Reality Itself.

Whatever apparently arises "objectively"—whether apparently "within" or apparently "without"—<u>Is</u> Only (and Only apparently) a Self-modification of the Transcendental Spiritual Self-Radiance of the One and Indivisible Conscious

Light That Is the Intrinsic Self-Nature, Self-Condition, and Self-State of Reality Itself.

The Self-Existing, Self-Radiant, and Self-Conscious Light That Is Reality Itself Is egoless, Indivisible, Non-separate, and Perfectly Acausal Real God.

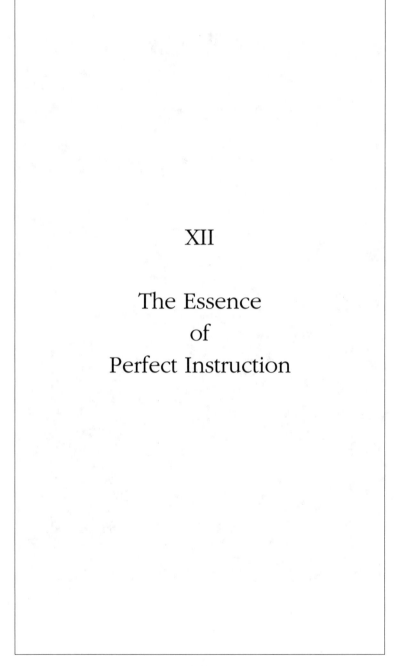

XII

The Essence
of
Perfect Instruction

Reality Itself <u>Is</u> Intrinsically (or Always Already) Self-Evident and egolessly all-and-All-Pervading.

Then why is the egoless Self-Nature, Self-Condition, and Self-State of Reality Itself not Self-Realized by one and all?

The <u>only</u> "reason why" the egoless Self-Nature, Self-Condition, and Self-State of Reality Itself is not Self-Realized in any instance is ego-"I"—or "point of view".

Therefore, the egoless Self-Nature, Self-Condition, and Self-State of Reality Itself can indeed <u>Be</u> Self-Realized by any one at all—simply by Standing Perfectly Prior to ego-"I", or "point of view".

That is to say, Self-Realization of the egoless Self-Nature, Self-Condition, and Self-State of Reality Itself is not possible by turning "out"—or toward any "<u>object</u>" of ego-"I", or of "point of view".

Self-Realization of the egoless Self-Nature, Self-Condition, and Self-State of Reality Itself <u>Is</u> Perfectly Prior to "within", Perfectly Prior to dissociative introversion, Perfectly Prior to seeking toward any "inner object", and Perfectly Prior to seeking toward any "outer object".

Self-Realization of the egoless Self-Nature, Self-Condition, and Self-State of Reality Itself <u>Is</u> Always Already <u>In</u> <u>Place</u>, <u>As</u> <u>Is</u>, Perfectly Prior to ego-"I", or "point of view"—and Always Already Perfectly Prior to all "objects" (whether "inner" or "outer"), and Always Already Perfectly Prior to all seeking toward "objects" (whether "inner" or "outer").

Self-Realization of the egoless Self-Nature, Self-Condition, and Self-State of Reality Itself <u>Is</u> in moment to moment Self-Abiding <u>As</u> <u>Is</u>—Perfectly Prior to <u>all</u> "objects", and Always Already <u>As</u> That Self-Nature, Self-Condition, and Self-State That is not an "object".

Self-Realization of the egoless Self-Nature, Self-Condition, and Self-State of Reality Itself <u>Is</u> "Where" no ego-"I", or "point of view", or any kind of "object" arises.

Such <u>Is</u> "Perfect Knowledge".

The Practice of "Perfect Knowledge" <u>Is</u>, Itself, Most Perfect when, in and by Means of ego-transcending devotional Communion with Me, the egoless Self-Realization of the Self-Nature, Self-Condition, and Self-State of Reality Itself <u>Is</u> Demonstrated to <u>Be</u> Transcendentally Spiritually "Bright", Full, and all-and-All-Outshining.

To order
books, tapes, CDs, DVDs, and videos by and about
His Divine Presence Ruchira Avatar Adi Da Samraj,
contact the Dawn Horse Press:

1-877-770-0772 (from within North America)

1-707-928-6653 (from outside North America)

Or visit the Dawn Horse Press website:

www.dawnhorsepress.com

Find out more about His Divine Presence Ruchira Avatar Adi Da Samraj and the Reality-Way of Adidam

■ Find out about courses, seminars, events, and retreats by calling the regional center nearest you.

AMERICAS
12040 N. Seigler Rd.
Middletown, CA
95461 USA
1-707-928-4936

THE UNITED KINGDOM
uk@adidam.org
0845-330-1008

EUROPE-AFRICA
Annendaalderweg 10
6105 AT Maria Hoop
The Netherlands
31 (0)20 468 1442

PACIFIC-ASIA
12 Seibel Road
Henderson
Auckland 0614
New Zealand
64-9-838-9114

AUSTRALIA
P.O. Box 244
Kew 3101
Victoria
**1800 ADIDAM
(1800-234-326)**

INDIA
F-168 Shree Love-Ananda Marg
Rampath, Shyam Nagar Extn.
Jaipur - 302 019, India
91 (141) 2293080

EMAIL: **correspondence@adidam.org**

■ Order books, tapes, CDs, DVDs, and videos by and about Ruchira Avatar Adi Da Samraj.

1-877-770-0772 (from within North America)
1-707-928-6653 (from outside North America)
order online: **www.dawnhorsepress.com**

■ Visit the Adidam website:
www.adidam.org

Discover more about His Divine Presence Ruchira Avatar Adi Da Samraj and the Reality-Way of Adidam.